GOD & COUNTRY
FOREVER

PAUL REVERE O'MARY

TATE PUBLISHING & *Enterprises*

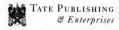
TATE PUBLISHING
& Enterprises

Tate Publishing is committed to excellence in the publishing industry. Our staff of highly trained professionals, including editors, graphic designers, and marketing personnel, work together to produce the very finest books available. The company reflects the philosophy established by the founders, based on Psalms 68:11,

"THE LORD GAVE THE WORD AND GREAT WAS THE COMPANY OF THOSE WHO PUBLISHED IT."

If you would like further information, please contact us:
1.888.361.9473 | www.tatepublishing.com
TATE PUBLISHING & Enterprises, LLC | 127 E. Trade Center Terrace
Mustang, Oklahoma 73064 USA

God and Country Forever

Published in the United States of America

ISBN: 978-1-5988670-3-9

07.03.14

This book is dedicated to my wife, Jane Marie, daughters Mary Allean, Sharon Leigh, and Karen Marie, to my departed parents, William Thomas O'Mary and Leona Beatrice O'Mary, to my brothers, Henry Lloyd and William Thomas, Jr., and to my sister, Ethel Mae O'Mary Boshell—all with whom I will share eternity.

TABLE OF CONTENTS

ACKNOWLEDGEMENTS

A LOT OF PEOPLE, LIVING AND DEAD HAVE touched my life. My dad, William Thomas O'Mary, was chief among them. He taught me things about living that one could never learn in school. He was the first to introduce me to the Bible and Christ Jesus. My commitment to the ideals and principles that made America great came from him. I owe him and my mother, Leona Beatrice Dudley O'Mary, everything for directing my path at an early time in life. I owe teachers like Kate Shaw and Mary Clifford Ray of Carbon Hill, Alabama. These great teachers found a way to push knowledge through a thick skull and show me the path to learning. They opened a lot of doors and enticed me to enter. At this writing, they have long departed for the Great Classroom in the Sky, and I hope that this word of eternal gratitude will drift upward to be shared posthumously by two of the greatest teachers to ever hold a piece of chalk.

I owe much to another great teacher, now officially retired but still teaching. Being a little older than she, it was not my privilege to be a student in her classroom. As fortune would have it, she became my daughter Karen's mother-in-law, and through that relationship I learned of her depth of knowledge and dedication to helping young people realize the fullness of their potential. She is Carolyn Spann, and I leaned heavily on her inspiration in writing this book.

Making the Army my chosen profession was easy, thanks to First Lieutenant (later Colonel) William C. Wood, my Company Commander in Company L, 19th Infantry, 24th

COLONEL "DOAK" WALKER

Infantry Division—part of 8th Army that occupied Japan at the end of World War II. He was one of the most inspirational leaders I've ever known. Instead of trying to get me to re-enlist, he persuaded me to take a discharge, get a college degree, and come back in the Army as an officer. I heeded his counsel, and he owns my eternal gratitude.

DR. CECIL RANDALL

The inspiration to write this book came primarily from my family and from some of the closest friends that man could have upon the earth—Prayer Partners Reverend Vial Fontenot, Grady Friday, Lanny Gamble, Rick Gibson, Bob Gross, George Hamner, Milton Marcum, Doug McElvy, Tom Myers, Don Norton, Harvey Stell, Jerry Thomas, and Reverend Carl Wells. For over two decades, we have met

DR. RICK LANCE

weekly at an early morning hour, shared our concerns, bared our very souls, confided in each other, laughed together, and prayed together. Then, there were the

A Few of the Great Soldiers History Should Remember

 Colonel Harry A. "Paddy" Flint, Commander of the 39th Infantry Regiment during WWII in North Africa, painted "AAA-O" (acronym of Anywhere Anytime Anyplace Bar Nothing) on his helmet that became the regiment's motto, killed in action on the Normandy Beachhead in June of 1944.

 Lt. Colonel William "Bill" Gore, one of the Army's all-time most audacious soldiers, received a battlefield commission in WWII, contracted polio while commanding a ranger company behind enemy lines in Korea but rescued successfully under cover of darkness, member of the Ranger Hall of Fame.

 Colonel Ralph Puckett, first commander of the Mountain Ranger Camp at Dahlonega, Georgia, courageous combat leader in Korean Conflict and Vietnam War, soldier's soldier held in the highest esteem army-wide, member of the Ranger Hall of Fame, always left a pair of boots too large for his successor.

 Colonel John F. "Skip" Sadler, one of the most universally respected and duty-driven soldiers to ever wear the uniform, first person to ever be snatched off the ground by a fixed-wing aircraft, airborne infantryman by nature and by choice, commanded at all levels commensurate with his rank, including command of SOG during Vietnam War.

LT. GENERAL HENRY E. "HANK" EMERSON, one of the best battlefield commanders of our time with magnificent sustained record of success in both Korea and Vietnam, fighting and winning with the least possible loss of human life, literally loved by his men.

CHARLES "CHUCK" WISE, soldier and super patriot; was to general "Hank" Emerson in Vietnam what Tonto was to the Lone Ranger, not atypical of legions of nameless young American soldiers whose commitment to duty, honor, country held no limits.

COLONEL WILLIAM E. "BILL" WEBER, only double-amputee ever retained on active duty, 11th Airborne Division in WWII, awesome leader, lost arm and leg about 30 minutes apart in Korea, special award of Distinguished Service Medal while serving on the Army General Staff, President of the American Airborne Association, Editor of Airborne Quarterly.

GENERAL JOHN R. "UNCLE JACK" DEANE, one of the army's all-time great combat leaders, extensive combat experience in WWII and Vietnam, loved by his men, commanded at every level, including the 173rd Airborne Brigade in Vietnam and the 82nd Airborne Division at Fort Bragg, North Carolina.

COLONEL LLOYD L. SCOOTER BURKE, audacious commander and recipient of the Congressional Medal of Honor for action above and beyond the call of duty while serving in Korea, most decorated soldier in the war, loved by his men, highly respected by all who knew him, played a drum in his high school band.

MAJOR GENERAL CHARLIE ROGERS, audacious commander and recipient of the Congressional Medal of Honor for action above and beyond the call of duty while serving in Vietnam, loved immensely by his men and highly respected by all who knew him, a truly great American soldier.

GENERAL LOUIS WILSON, looked upon by many as the greatest Marine who ever lived, former Commandant of the Marine Corps, recipient of the Congressional Medal of Honor, surely one of the most admired and respected military leaders to ever wear the uniform.

LT. GENERAL HAROLD "HAL" MOORE, Commander of two rifle companies in Korea and a battalion and brigade in Vietnam, principal participant in first major battle of Vietnam War as commander of the 1st Battalion, 7th Cavalry, played by Mel Gibson in the magnificent movie, "We Were Soldiers."

COLONEL ELLIOTT P. "BUD" SYDNOR, esteemed Airborne Ranger, airborne battalion commander in Vietnam, Ranger School Commandant, member of the Ranger Hall of Fame and Son Tay Raid (prisoner of war rescue incursion into North Vietnam).

COMMAND SERGEANT MAJOR JAMES J. "JIM" GALLAGHER, a magnificent soldier, talented writer and inspirational leader, author of *Low Intensity Conflict* and the *10th Edition of Combat Leader's Field Guide,* one of the two best NCOS the author ever knew.

COMMAND SERGEANT MAJOR CURTIS DUCO, one of a few soldiers to earn the Combat Infantryman's Badge in three wars, one of the best soldiers, officer or enlisted, to wear the uniform in 228 years of Army history, and one of the two best NCOS the author observed in over 30 years of service.

LT. GENERAL JAMES F. HOLLINGSWORTH, distinguished battlefield leader, served in three wars-- World War II, Korea, and with 1st Infantry Division (Big Red One) in Vietnam – loved by his men, honored by Texas A & M University as one of its all-time greatest graduates.

LT. GENERAL WILLIAM "BILL" CARPENTER, courageous combat leader, called the "lonesome end" on Army football team, participant in some of the most intense combat in the Vietnam War, one of the most universally respected General Officers of our time.

THE SULLIVAN BROTHERS

Joseph, Frank, Albert, Madison, and George (above L to R) – of Waterloo, Iowa, volunteered for Navy in WWII, perished when their ship, the USS Juneau, was torpedoed by the Japanese at Guadalcanal, the greatest loss of the members of one family in Navy History.

ABOUT THE AUTHOR

PAUL REVERE O'MARY IS A VETERAN OF OVER 32 years of Army service. He volunteered for the Army near the end of hostilities in World War II, served in the 19th Infantry Regiment, 24th Infantry Division, one of the units to occupy Japan at the end of the war. He became a non-commissioned officer but took a discharge when his term-of-service expired to attend college, acquire a Regular Army Commission, and re-enter the Army as an officer. He saw combat as an Infantry Officer in the Korean Conflict and subsequently served three years as an Instructor of Leadership at Fort Benning, Georgia. He served for two years in the Third Infantry (President's Honor Guard), was the Operations Officer of both the G-2 and G-3 Divisions of Berlin Brigade during the building of the wall, served three years as an Assignment Officer in Infantry Branch, saw combat as an Infantry officer in Vietnam during a period that included the Tet Offensive of 1968, and subsequently served four years in the Pentagon with the Army General Staff and Joint Chiefs of Staff.

He is a graduate of the Command and General Staff College, the Armed Forces Staff College, and the Army War College, holds an advanced degree from George Washington University, and presently serves as Honorary Colonel of the 58th Infantry, a proud regiment to which he gave the name of "Patriots" during the Vietnam War. He ended his military career as Professor of Military Science at the University of Alabama, building the size of the cadet corps from 150 to over 2,200 during a period of great anti-military sentiment on the nation's college campuses. Subsequent to his retirement as a Colonel in 1978, he served 10 years as a University Administrator and a part-time Professor of Human Resources Management in the College of Commerce and Business Administration at the University of Alabama.

Among his many U.S. and foreign military awards and decorations are two awards of the Combat Infantryman's Badge, Purple Heart, and Distinguished Service Medal, being one of a very few officers below general officer grade to receive this high award since its establishment by Congress in 1918.

Colonel O'Mary and his wife, Jane Marie, make their home in Tuscaloosa, Alabama.

DR. GILMAN
McKEE

COLONEL GEORGE
HODGSON

JAMES SPANN

TOM MYERS

encouraging words from a host of great soldiers, particularly Lt. General Henry E. "Hank" Emerson and Colonel Robert E. "Doak" Walker, and from a former soldier in the ranks, Charles "Chuck" Wise, a Vietnam veteran, later gravely wounded as a guard on the Mexican border, and at this writing is serving a second time in Iraq in a dangerous undertaking.

I acknowledge the spiritual food that it has been my good fortune to feed upon for the past 28 years—food that came from the messages, challenges, and examples of such great pastors as Drs. Cecil Randall, Rick Lance, Gilman McKee, and from my dear friend, Retired Army Colonel George Hodgson, a gifted scholar and Bible teacher, versed as few are in the Scriptures.

Given the inspiration and encouragement that have come from so many, neither this book nor the American Patriotism Association (APA) would exist without the technical expertise and effort of James Spann, first President of the APA and one of the nation's most distinguished meteorologists and TV personalities. I owe much to my dear friends—Kathy Rice, John Myers, and Gary Shores—whose technical skills have been invaluable to me from the moment I began writing and assembling this book. I offer my most profound gratitude to my special friend Tom Myers—great American, super patriot, dedicated community servant, educator, inspirational leader, role model, and prayer partner—whose inspiration is reflected in much of the substance of this book. Lastly, I express my everlasting gratitude to Roy & Nona Crowder, Reverend Bob and Barbara Gladney, Don & Nancy Norton, Bert and Julie Guy, Rich and Cheri Wingo, and Tommy and Robin Ford—great Americans, special friends, and faithful servants of Jesus Christ whose leadership and Christian example have contributed so greatly to God's kingdom and to the effectiveness and unity of our local church. Their moral courage, impeccable character, unselfish service, and daily walk reflect the kind of citizenship this book seeks to promote and foster throughout our beloved land.

I have asked God to bless the words that appear here—to guide my hand across each new line I write. Much of what you'll read was written over a period of years, and I ask His blessings on all of it, having faith that what He blesses will achieve the purpose for which it was intended. I acknowledge Him as my Lord and my God and thank Him on behalf of Americans everywhere for what this book might do to help build a stronger, safer and better America.

PREFACE

"I would never want to be remembered for the wealth that I acquired or the personal profit I gained from life. Rather, I want to be remembered for that which I gave to help make a better way of life for mankind. Pity those who pity the soldier in our so-called self-sacrifice, for only those men and women who seek and understand a higher goal of life can have the realization that there is no such thing as self-sacrifice in the service of one's country. There is only self-achievement."

—Colonel William E. Weber, U.S. Army, Retired
(Double Amputee), Editor-in-Chief, *Airborne Magazine*

THIS BOOK HAS BEEN DESIGNED TO HELP YOU TO be a great American. Master its content and let the things it espouses guide your life, and you can't help but reach a new level of self-achievement. It will enable some of you to reach the pinnacle of your chosen professions. For others of you, the words in this book will bring a new and higher quality of life, prepare you to help raise the moral fiber of our land, and assist you in helping to build a stronger, safer, and better America. We need to do this if the American way of life is to survive and prevail.

The last half-century has seen a profound decline in our nation's dedication to the ideals and principles embraced so deeply by the American people prior to and during World War II. Most of the two generations of Americans living during the Great Depression, who paid the monumental price that was necessary for victory in World War II, found themselves unable to instill the same degree of commitment in the hearts and minds of their children, the post-war "baby boomers." Instead, they watched the family unit deteriorate as their children left home for college or found work in distant locations and embraced an individual lifestyle that in more cases than not differed from their upbringing. Prodigal plenty abounded, and materialism found its way into what was left of the family household. Social Studies replaced Civics and Democracy in grade school, and two decades later, too many Americans had grown ignorant of our system of government and our individual responsibilities to it—a troubling fact that would contribute to our national unraveling during the Vietnam War and now threatens our efforts to bring freedom, peace, and stability to the Middle East. This troubling condition prompts me to mention certain aspects of our system of government in the preface to this book.

The United States of America was founded as a republic—a nation in which power rests with those citizens who are entitled to vote. This does not always mean that the majority will rule. Instead, power is generally exercised by elected or appointed officials who may side with or rule in favor of a minority opinion, position, or interest. Therefore, the United States is not a true democracy. A court of law consisting of a few people or in some cases a single Federal judge may decide in favor of a person or group that represents a very small minority of the nation's electorate. The Supreme Court's decision to ban teacher-led prayer from public schools and the Ninth Circuit Court of Appeals ruling to uphold the decision of a lower court that removes "under God" from the Pledge of Allegiance are examples of minority rule. This could never happen in a pure majority-rule democracy, but it is a practical possibility in a republic.

Despite any advantage or attractiveness that a pure majority-rule democracy may hold, it has a major shortcoming in the modern world. As the time available to react to human events moves closer and closer to zero, a pure democracy becomes an increasingly impractical system of government.

It is quite clear that the founding fathers realized that all decisions of government cannot wait on a vote of the people. So, they wove into its system the necessary implied powers for the President and other duly-elected representatives of the people to act immediately on matters that cannot wait. The elected officials of government do this with the realization that they represent all of the American people—not just those who voted them into office. The President and all other elected representatives at the state and national level owe the same allegiance to every person they represent, regardless of how a particular person may have voted. This distinguishes a republic from all other systems of government, and an understanding of its working parts and commitment to it are essential to the building of a stronger, safer, and better America.

A republican form of government is not without inherent imperfections, the judiciary processes of government being the most notable. Unlike the Executive and Legislative Branches of government, the Judicial Branch at the national level is immune to the electoral process by the public at large. A Supreme Court Justice can be removed involuntarily only by impeachment, and this is the underlying reason why confirmation of a nominee to the Court is one of the most difficult and contentious processes in all of government. It is the duty of the Justice to interpret the law and rule on the constitutionality of laws that affect Americans in so many different ways. When a vacancy on the Supreme Court occurs by reason of death or resignation, a monumental political fight is certain to develop among opposing interests, each member of the House and Senate apparently being convinced that a nominee's ideological bias too often holds dominion over his or her ability to objectively interpret the law. Unfortunately, the history of the Supreme Court tends to confirm this belief. Thus, the system is admittedly less than perfect, but it is still the best on our planet.

That the system has its imperfections is universally recognized, but it has stood the test of two centuries with no one offering a better alternative. As an example, the election of Supreme Court Justices by a popular vote of the people would likely result in chaos—if not outright anarchy. Imagine a general election of Supreme Court Justices where resolution of Roe versus Wade, prayer in public schools, and similar emotional issues rested on the outcome. At the same time, we have recognized that as good as a republican form of government has proven to be, it can be misunderstood, misused, and misapplied; and inequality can be created where equality was intended.

Such is the case in the classrooms of public schools across America where Evolution is taught freely as part of the Science curriculum, but God's name goes unmentioned. The act of the Supreme Court to ban teacher-led prayer from the campuses of public schools is no longer restricted to its original scope. Darwinist professors and the law makers who support them are somehow succeeding in bringing the teaching of Creation by Intelligent Design under the same umbrella, contending it would be equally offensive to teacher-led prayer. Part of their ploy is to deny that Atheism is a religion, disputing the truth of the aphorism: *Disbelieving something is tantamount to believing in its opposite.* Evolution, they contend, is a required part of the Science curriculum, part and parcel of the search for truth, and should not be relegated to an elective category.

While Darwinist professors would readily oppose government rule by oligarchy for the nation as a whole, they demand it for themselves in the classroom under the Holy Grail of academic freedom in which they are free to decide the content of the lesson plan. Thus, the academic floor is not level, and nothing good can result from the inequity. At an early time, the nation's courts of justice must come to grips with the question of what is good for America—a Darwin atheistic pagan society or freedom of choice and freedom of speech in the classroom.

Any system of government, regardless of the good things it holds, cannot necessarily ensure its own survival. A democracy, for example, must draw life from all of the people. Otherwise, it will die and pass into oblivion. The same can be said of a republic, for which "a refined democracy" might be a more descriptive title. Its survival rests upon an unwavering commitment of the American people *"to love it, to support its Constitution, to obey its laws, to respect its flag, and to defend it against all enemies"*—words contained in "The American's Creed," written by William Tyler Page in 1917 and accepted by the House of Representatives on 3 April 1918. A stronger, safer, and better America is not possible unless the American people can collectively and in concert impress these words upon our hearts and minds and obey them faithfully, fervently, consistently, and loyally.

One of the primary purposes of this book is to provide a catalyst to the American Patriotism Association (APA), a not-for-profit corporation designed and intended to help build a stronger, safer, and better America. The Association's goal is to identify and enroll each citizen of the United States who professes to be a patriotic American, loyal to the nation's institutions and ideals, a law-abiding citizen, and a person of impeccable moral character, committed to preserving our way of life for Americans yet unborn. The way to become a member of the APA is contained in this book's addendum.

The motto of the American Patriotism Association is "God and Country Forever," and it is the fervent cry of the Association for all of God-believing America to join in the crusade to rebuild the eroded moral fiber of our land.

Restoring the moral fiber of America will require a concerted effort of the people. In his "Gettysburg Address," President Lincoln described our system of government as being *"of the people, by the people, and for the people."* Even though America was engaged in a war against itself, Lincoln reminded us that America was *"conceived in liberty"* and called the war a test of *"whether this nation or any nation so conceived and so dedicated can long endure."* In the seven score years since those words were spoken, America has learned that a nation *"conceived in liberty"* can endure as long as *liberty* is not taken from the people. The words "freedom of religion" does not mean "freedom from religion," nor did it ever. The words "religious liberty" could just as easily have been used. The meaning is the same, and to take that away from the people is to destroy the cornerstone on which the nation was founded.

Being an American patriot will never be a bed of roses. There is a price to pay for being able to live as free people in a land where there are no restrictions on one's intellects or their energies—and where there's complete freedom to exercise the abilities we possess. Americans are free to choose a field of endeavor that is soul-satisfying, that contributes to the common good, and offers an opportunity for complete self-realization.

No other nation on earth can promise such an opportunity to every citizen. The United States of America can, but there are forces afoot on Planet Earth who seek to take that away. Someone must pay a price to see that they don't succeed, and it is the true patriots who end up being the ones to do almost all of the paying. It is a comforting truth that no nation or groups of nations can conquer America if all of our people can be persuaded to live and perform as Americans should, and therein rests the foremost reason for writing this book.

The pages that follow comprise a compilation of articles, speeches, documentaries, and vignettes that pertain to God and Country. In some way, each of them prepares the reader to play a part in helping to build an economically stronger, more patriotic, morally upright, and godly America. It is a manual that teaches the reader how to lead, how to live, the ways of responsible citizenship, the true meaning of patriotism, and how to serve God and Country.

Publication of this book is an old soldier's last act of service to my God and my Country. The worth of its words is all I have left to give.

I ask you to begin this book by opening your heart and soul to its substance. It begins with the best side of America speaking about herself. Most likely, you will find that it puts a lump in your throat and a tear in your eye. If so, feel good about it, because that's what it's supposed to do to every red-blooded American.

"I Am the United States of America" has been written and punctuated for use as a dramatic presentation at patriotic events and similar ceremonies.

I Am the United States of America

I was born in arms, purged in blood, made secure by sacrifice, and kept free by the grace of God.

If the great nation that is the United States of America could speak to the world in the way that she speaks to the hearts of American patriots everywhere, she would tell a story unique to recorded history. What follows is a part of that story—an effort by the author to capture the spirit of America, the things for which she stands, and impart the legacy of those who have lived and died to make the United States of America the greatest and most beloved nation to ever exist upon the earth.

I AM THE UNITED STATES OF AMERICA, AND I AM A nation under God. For more than two centuries, I have lived in freedom, because I have treasured liberty enough to defend it with my blood. From the moment of my birth, I have been the world's best hope of freedom. Where people struggle to escape the chains of bondage, look for me to be there. I am the United States of America, *the land of the free and the home of the brave.* I carry freedom's banner—in the cause of justice and human dignity.

I brought freedom's banner to my shores and planted it at Jamestown and Plymouth Rock. Short of the bare essentials of life, I suffered greatly from hunger and exposure in the untamed wilderness of my new land, but I survived—with God's help and in freedom's name.

Holding *these truths to be self-evident,* I asserted my right to live in freedom. My stated claim of the unalienable rights to *life, liberty, and the pursuit of happiness* embodied in my Declaration of Independence on that July 4, 1776 was a landmark in human history, but freedom remained to be won by blood, sweat, tears, and the shout of victory.

From that first day, *Liberty* was my battle cry, and I learned early of its monumental price. I stood and delivered at Lexington, Concord, and Bunker Hill, and the world learned that the price of freedom was a price I'd pay. I am the United States of America.

Hungry, cold, without shoes and adequate winter clothing, a third of my small army died at Valley Forge from exposure, disease, and starvation, but their sacrifice kindled their fervor and deepened the flame of freedom. Emerging from that awful winter with a burning zeal for independence, my determined ill-equipped soldiers fought on doggedly. Finally, on that historic day of October 19, 1781, at Yorktown, Virginia, the sunlight glinted from the sword and I—bleeding, begrimed, and battered—saw a nation born. From that moment in history, the bloodlines of the world have run through my veins, because I offered freedom's new home to the oppressed and the suffering, and they came and dwelt in my land.

I am the United States of America. I am 280 million

people and the legacy of millions who have given their all for me. I am Crispus Attucks, Nathan Hale, Stephen Decatur, and Paul Revere. I am George Washington, Thomas Jefferson, Abraham Lincoln, and Teddy Roosevelt. I am Patrick Henry, Benjamin Franklin, and Betsy Ross. I am Andrew Jackson and Woodrow Wilson, Ulysses S. Grant and Robert E. Lee. I am Geronimo, Chief Crazy Horse, and Sitting Bull. I am Colin Kelly and Rodger Young, Amelia Earhart and Charles Lindbergh. I am Franklin Roosevelt, John F. Kennedy, and Ronald Reagan. I am Booker T. Washington, Horace Greeley, Luther Burbank and George Washington Carver. I am George C. Marshall, Douglas MacArthur, and "Blackjack" Pershing, Audie Murphy and Alvin York. I am Omar Bradley, George Patton, Chester Nimitz, "Hap" Arnold, and a man called "Ike." I am the Daughters of the American Revolution, Veterans of Foreign Wars, the American Legion, and a nameless hero that history failed to remember.

Hardship and suffering have weighted my steps but taught me to persevere and endure. I paid a price to win my freedom, only to see the next generation of my people shed their blood to keep it. The Redcoat returned to my shores, but at New Orleans the sound of my musketry silenced the British drum and showed again the price I'd pay to keep my liberty. The British and soon the world would learn that fighting blood flows through the veins of the United States of America.

My tiny, determined army had banished the foreign foe from my land, but there would be growing pains before I came of age. Short of essentials but formidable in spirit, my tiny army turned its head westward, serving as scout, guard, warrior, and peacemaker. Too small to be called an army, these brave men learned to measure their worth—not in terms of bravery and fighting skill which they owned in great abundance—but in terms of their ability to persevere and endure. They endured—not for glory or reward—but to keep the settler safe and move freedom's border westward to the Pacific Ocean. These brave men and the generation to follow planted my flag throughout the west, fighting a bloody war with Mexico, perishing gallantly at the Alamo, but winning independence for the Republic of Texas. I annexed Texas to my union and came of age.

Then suddenly my world was jolted at Fort Sumter, Bull Run, Shiloh, Fredericksburg, Chancellorsville, Gettysburg, Vicksburg, Petersburg—both north and south across my land. From Manassas to Appomattox, I fought and bled—brother against brother, friend against friend. Some wore blue and some wore gray, but the color of the mud and the color of the blood held sway. Facing my darkest hour, *I followed two flags, but united them strong and proved my nation could right a wrong*—and long endure—with God's help and in freedom's name.

The pages of history do not record a war fought with such tenacity as the one among my people, and its painful memory across my battered land had not subsided when I answered a neighbor's cry for freedom. On 1 July 1898, I drove the invader from San Juan Hill, broke the bastion at Santiago, and freed my Cuban neighbor from Spanish tyranny. The war against the Spanish invader showed the world that my people would shed their precious blood for the freedom of all mankind—both within and beyond our beloved shores. But the tyrant is slow to learn. Less than two decades later, I answered freedom's call far beyond my shores, halted the onslaught of the German Hun, and surged forward. *I cracked the Hindenburg Line, broke the Kaiser's spine, and didn't come back 'til it was over over there.*

A generation older and hardened by the Great Depression that brought great suffering and hardship across the length and breadth of my land, my people needed a time of peace more than ever in their history—but it was not to be. The tyrant struck again, and it fell my lot to cross the English Channel, breach the strong beach defenses, fight through the hedgerows, liberate the French nation, *break out at St. Lo,* where I lost 10,000 of my beloved sons in a single day, *and swarm the German heartland.* The Third Reich had misjudged the United States of America, and Hitler's dream of a master race and world domination died on that VE Day in 1945. On almost every island in the Pacific, I met the foe—nose-to-nose, eyeball-to-eyeball, and blood-to-blood. I gave ground briefly to his greater numbers, but I rallied with resolve and returned with vengeance. My bombers rained destruction on the Japanese homeland, and in the great sea battles of Midway, Leyte Gulf, and the Coral Sea, I made the enemy pay dearly for Pearl Harbor. I broke through his strong deliberate defenses on Iwo Jima, *planted Old Glory on the summit of Mount Suribachi,* and looked northward. In the greatest battle for an island in all of history, over 40,000 of my beloved sons were killed or wounded in the incredible land, air, and sea battle for Okinawa. The cost was heavy, but my great victory ended the dreams of Hirohito and his imperial Japanese Empire—and *set the Rising Sun*. I replaced tyranny with democracy, assisted in raising the Japanese standard of living to the highest level in its history, and have since protected her people's freedom for over a half-century.

The fall of Germany and the unconditional surrender of Japan ended a mighty war that involved almost every nation on earth and took the lives of over 400,000 Americans. The cost was monumental, but hope prevailed for an era of peace in a world without war. North Korea and Communist China ended that hope five years later, and I once again answered freedom's call. Over 34,000 of my beloved sons would give their lives on the Korean Peninsula to restore the sovereignty and freedom of a small agrarian nation that could offer me nothing but gratitude in return.

Then, now, and always, my fallen soldiers are the first among my people to receive my homage and honor. Rather than leave them where they fall, I spill my blood, if necessary, to retrieve my fallen comrades so that they might rest in their hallowed silent bivouacs. I am Arlington National Cemetery, the Tomb of the Unknowns, the missing-in-action, and the folded flag presented to a Gold Star Mother on behalf of the President of the United States and the people of a grateful nation.

I am the spirit of the human heart, the hope that never dies, and the indomitable spirit that drives me onward to unwavering perseverance. I am the will to win and the determination to succeed. I am a people endowed with a special quality—a quality that cannot be seen and cannot be touched—but something so completely real that it makes up the very soul of my people. It is a quality that brings victory in the fourth quarter—a quality that produces uncommon sacrifice—and a quality that sometimes brings the sober and humble realization that "there but for the grace of God go I."

I am the oil fields of Texas and Oklahoma, the wheat fields of Kansas and Missouri, the corn fields of Iowa and Nebraska, the bluegrass of Kentucky, the skyscrapers of New York and Chicago, and the coal fields of the Virginias, Alabama, and Pennsylvania. I am the fertile lands of the Sun Belt, the Grand Canyon, and the Golden Gate. I am the Statue of Liberty, Independence Hall, and the Washington Monument. I am the mighty Mississippi and the Florida Everglades, the western prairies, the ski slopes of Colorado, the Rocky Mountains, and the incoming tides breaking on my shores. I am a walk through the woods, a stroll through the garden, and the trickle of a mountain stream.

No nation on earth can equal the beauty of my landscape, and only I among nations can boast of having every climate on earth. I am three million square miles of scenic beauty implanted between the world's two largest oceans. Alaska and Hawaii lie separated from my inner shores, yet cohesively woven into my inseparable union—not because of military conquest—but because it was the fervent plea of the people of these beautiful lands to become part of the United States of America.

You can look at me and see the fulfillment of the human dream. You can look at me and see what sacrifice and human effort have made possible. You can see why my people thank God for having been born an American and why so many millions of the people of other nations seek to live in my land. You can look at me and see a nation worth every sacrifice that my people are called upon to make. God truly shed His grace upon the United States of America.

I am Babe Ruth, Hank Aaron, Dizzy Dean, Ty Cobb, Ted Williams, and the World Series. I am Jackie Robinson, the Four Horsemen, the Galloping Ghost, and the Super Bowl. I am Michael Jordan and Larry Bird, Jesse Owens, Jim Thorpe, and Joe Louis. I am Ben Hogan, Arnold Palmer, Jack Nicklaus, and Tiger Woods. I am Eddie Arcaro, Willie Shoemaker, and the Kentucky Derby. I am the Indianapolis 500, the Boston Marathon, and the Final Four. I am the roar of a crowd in a stadium, Bear Bryant leaning on a goalpost, a goal at the buzzer, and a game-saving goal line stand.

I am the United States of America, where the well-being and quality of life of my people transcend the power of government. I am the watchful eye of the public servant, an ominous weather warning, and a recreation center. I am Walter Reed and Jonas Salk, a local hospital, and the Mayo Clinic. I am a song book and a symphony orchestra, Oscar Hammerstein and Irving Berlin, Glenn Miller and Tommy Dorsey, Van Cliburn and Elvis Presley, Bill Gaither, a gospel quartet, and the chime of bells on a Sunday morning.

I am Thomas Edison and Henry Ford, Albert Einstein and Eli Whitney. I am Billy Graham, Fulton Sheen, and Martin Luther King. I am Walt Disney, Will Rogers, and John Wayne, David Brinkley, Paul Harvey, and Diane Sawyer. I am Walter Winchell, Bill Mauldin, and Ernie Pyle. I am John Glenn and Christa McAuliffe, Bill Gates, the

Internet, and an e-mail greeting from a far-away friend. I am the tulips of spring and the colors of fall, the sound of a locomotive, the song of a mocking bird, and the warmth of the family circle at eventide.

Yes, I am the United States of America, the greatest nation to ever exist upon the earth—and around the world I stand in defense of freedom and as a living deterrent to war and bloodshed. In freedom's cause, for nearly half a century, I have stood beside my friends at the 38th parallel in Korea. In Germany, for five decades, I have protected the very nation that tried to bring the world under its domination. In Berlin, for three decades, I watched a nation imprison itself by walling off its only avenue to freedom, and I looked on with tears of joy as that infamous wall found its place in history among the rubble of monuments built to the cruelty of mankind.

Peace and freedom are at the apex of the things I treasure most, and I lead the world in the effort to obtain them for all mankind. Yet, no generation of my people has escaped war, and in my hour of peril, I somehow find men of a special breed who step forward to answer my call—men like Colin Powell and Norman Schwarzkopf, and countless other great fighting men, unknown to most Americans, but who hold a special place in the hearts of those they marched among—men like Paddy Flint and Bill Gore, Ralph Puckett and "Skip" Sadler, "Gunfighter" Hank Emerson and Bill Weber, "Uncle Jack" Deane, "Scooter" Burke, and Charlie Rogers, Louis Wilson, Hal Moore, and Bud Sydnor, James Gallagher, Curtis Duco, and Jim Hollingsworth, Hugh and Ralph Pattillo, Bill Carpenter, the Sullivan Brothers, and millions of others, living and dead, for whom our nation, our American way of life, and the honorable profession of arms stand as their eternal monument. History may fail to record their names, but their legacy to the United States of America will live in perpetuity.

Wherever lies a challenge to the freedom of humankind, count on me to be there. I was there in the past. I am there now, and I will be there tomorrow. From Concord Bridge to the war in Iraq, I have taken charge by my physical presence upon the ground. That is the way it should be, and therein rests my destiny. I am the United States of America.

There have been times when I traveled uncharted paths, and there were times when my trumpet gave forth an uncertain sound. In Vietnam, I had to learn again that the further a nation is from the chains of bondage the less its people value their own freedom and the freedom of others. I had to learn again that my soldiers should never be required to fight and die in a war that the rules would not let them win. I had to learn again that the human right to freedom is shared by every inhabitant on earth, because it is God-given, and no tyrant has the right to take it away. I also had to remind myself that world leadership carries an obligation to protect the freedom of others far beyond my shores—that there is a monumental price to be paid in the cause of human liberty.

In Somalia, I had to learn again that the great nation that is the United States of America should never enter a conflict, even one of low intensity, without the presence of overwhelming combat power. Somalia and Grenada reminded me again that the tyrants of the world often turn a deaf ear to the diplomat but listen carefully to the American soldier. Moammar Qadaffi turned a deaf ear to my diplomatic effort but was persuaded to understand my airmailed message that the tyrants of the world will pay a price for trying to establish their own international law. Saddam Hussein ignored my diplomats but learned from my fighting men that the tyrant is not at liberty to take the freedom of a defenseless neighbor and threaten free people everywhere—and as those lessons were being learned, the would-be tyrants of the world stared in awe at the incomparable skill of my fighting men and took note of the swift and certain destruction that awaits the tyrant and the terrorist.

Let history forever record that it was my will and determination, my eternal vigilance, my demonstrated fighting skill, my ingenuity, my sacrifice, my staying power and perseverance—when other nations faltered and sometimes deserted me—my commitment to moral principle, my unwavering dedication to the cause of liberty, my commitment to "duty-honor-country," and my steadfast faith in a benevolent God that made shambles of the evil oppressive empire that was the Soviet Union—a momentous event in human history that forever laid bare the *Communist Manifesto* and *Das Kapital* for what they truly are—not a method or means for human betterment—but evil and cruel manuals on how to gain power and enslave the human race.

Yes, I am the United States of America, *the land of the free and the home of the brave*—a nation that was born in arms, purged in blood, and made secure by sacrifice—*a nation of the people, by the people, and for the people.*

In all of history there has been none other like me. I am a nation under God, sustained by a national commitment that His purpose shall truly be our own. From God Himself, I thus identify my national purpose—a purpose not given birth by my people—but by Him—a purpose to endure to the end of my longevity.

As the curtain opens on the 21st Century, it is my fervent prayer that my people will always possess the will, the determination, the moral fiber, and the strength of character to defend my freedom, wherever and whenever it is threatened. I pray fervently that my people will ever know and remember that *"Blessed is the nation whose God is the Lord"* and pray daily that freedom's rainbow will forever cast its arch across my land and that God will continue to bless the United States of America.

Soldier

The stars swing down the western steep,
And soon the east will burn with day;
And we shall struggle up from sleep,
And sling our packs and march away.
In this brief hour before the dawn
Has struck our bivouac with flame,
I think of men whose brows have borne
The deadly wreath of worldly fame.
I see the grizzled grenadier,
The dark dragoon, the gay Hussar,
Whose shoulders bore for many a year
Their little emperor's blazing star.
I see the fatal phalanx creep
Like death across the world and back—
With eyes that only strive to keep
Bucephalus' immortal track.
I see the horde of Genghis Khan
Spread outward like the dawn of day
To trample golden Korofan
And thunder over fair Cathay.
I see the legions wheel through Gaul,
The sword and flame on hearth and home
And all the men who had to fall
That Caesar might be first in Rome.
I see these things; yet am I slave
When banners flaunt and bugles blow;
Content to fill a soldier's grave
For reasons I shall never know.

Major General Charles T. "Buck" Lanham (1902–1976)

The history of civilization is the story of the leader and those who followed him. Mighty empires and great civilizations resulted from inspirational leadership and crumbled in its absence. The United States of America is no different. The extent of our longevity will also rest upon the grace of God and the quality of leadership that we are able to produce and maintain. Building a stronger, safer, and better America must start with the making of great leaders. Thus, "Only One Way to Lead" is the first instructional topic to appear in this book.

ONLY ONE WAY TO LEAD

Each step up the ladder of success is made possible by becoming over-qualified to stand on the rung where you now are.

FOR AMERICA TO REALIZE THE FULLNESS OF ITS potential, her citizenry must learn to follow and to lead. A large segment of our population is searching for good leadership—on the job and off the job. Regretfully, even larger numbers of our citizenry neither want to lead nor be led. One of the main goals of the American Patriotism Association is to help build great leadership and "followership" beginning with our youth and extending to all age groups of our society.

There are those who contend that leadership cannot be taught, and they have been able to convince a lot of people that they are right. However strong their arguments may appear, the facts show that leadership can be learned, and there is a sound basis for taking issue with those who contend that it cannot be taught. When a person of prominence makes an assertion, his words are footnoted by other writers, and as time passes, assertions become accepted facts. In too many instances, we confuse good leadership with position attainment and lend more credence to public utterances or the written word than the facts really merit.

Some persons in positions of high authority or great notoriety become self-appointed experts, when in fact they only have their ignorance organized a little better than others. Depending on the subject, their uttered opinions may do little damage, but in others the impact has been monumental. For example, the contention that pure 24-carat leadership cannot be taught has been embraced by academicians in higher education to such an extent that it finds no place in the curricula of the Colleges of Commerce and Business across the land. Our students are able to attend classes in *"human resources management," "business management," "personnel management," or just plain "management,"* but the content falls far short of pure 24-carat leadership training.

THE BASIC CONCEPT OF LEADERSHIP

Things were that way yesterday, but it is my fervent hope that for the reader of this treatise yesterday ended last night. Today is a new day, and the first order of business is to begin correcting the nation's leadership ills. We have to teach potential leaders how to lead and how to follow. There's a way to do that, and those learning the basic fundamental doctrine contained herein and then applying it to all they do in life will magnify their probability of reaching the pinnacle of their chosen profession. Now, if anyone thinks he or she can't do that, they're right. No one without complete confidence can reach such a level of attainment. But I hope you don't think you can't. Your attitude is your best friend or your worst enemy. So, the task you and I share is to cause you to be over-qualified in what you now do. Each step up the ladder of success is made possible by becoming over-qualified to stand on the rung where you now are. Unfortunately, our present problem exists in a large measure by the fact that the overwhelming majority of America's leaders are not over-qualified at any level, and every area of American life suffers from it. So, master what is written here, and I promise that you can be outstanding among the outstanding. If you have a burning desire to be that good and take it upon yourself to master the doctrine and apply it in your daily walk, you can be a singularly outstanding inspirational leader of other men and women.

The doctrine contained here is not available in a single cohesive package anywhere. It is thus my fervent hope that you will memorize this concept and teach it to others across America. I wish that the doctrine had existed when I was young and that someone had taught it to me so that I may have been able to use it. Unfortunately, a lot of my life had passed before I ever heard of a "Basic Concept of Leadership" that I could use to make me a better leader. After I did learn it, I profited from it greatly. It came too late for me to reach the pinnacle of my profession, but I could never have achieved what I did without being lucky enough to have been assigned to a position where I became associated with some of the very best leaders the nation had at that time. I learned a leadership doctrine, and it became second nature to me to apply it—and doing so enabled me to achieve things far beyond any expectations I might have had otherwise.

During the 1950s, I was fortunate enough to have served three years on the Leadership Committee of the Infantry School at Fort Benning, Georgia, where the "Basic Concept of Leadership" was developed and taught. I taught thousands of young officers who knew practically nothing about leading other men and women. They learned a concept of leadership that they were able to use when they assumed command of their own units after leaving Fort Benning. Some of the young Lieutenants who underwent the leadership training conducted during those years went on to be great Generals. They had learned some leadership during their pre-commission training, but each of them would tell you that they knew very little of how to lead other men the day they entered on active duty as commissioned officers. In short, leadership can be taught and it can be learned, but the correct basic doctrine must be learned at the outset. I contend that it is a fundamental truth of incontestable substance that there is only one correct concept of leadership into which all people can fit themselves. It is my purpose here to set forth that basic concept in writing.

THE DEFINITION OF LEADERSHIP

With that, let's talk about leadership, and the most logical approach is to begin with its definition. The definition has certain components that must be included if it is to be complete. First of all, ***leadership is an art*** and like any art, it can be learned and mastered by anyone who has a burning desire to be an outstanding leader of other people and takes it upon himself or herself to master that art. Surely, Peter's Principle applies here. There is a level beyond which some people may not progress. No matter how hard a moron may try, he or she could never lead an assembly of more intelligent people, but a moron could become a leader of other morons. The message here is that all can learn to lead and that no one is born knowing how to do it. Leaders are made—not born. Inherent within that statement is another fundamental truth that no type of personality is more suited to lead than another. People on opposite ends of the personality spectrum can be equally effective in leading other people. More on this assertion will be addressed later in this dissertation.

Now, though, let's go back and build on the definition of leadership. We've said that leadership is an art. So, let's go further and state that *leadership is the art of influencing and directing*. Everything we do or make it a point not to do either influences people positively or negatively. Inaction can be as influential as action. Every waking moment is important to the leader, because influence cannot be switched on and off like a light bulb. Every word we speak (or how we say it) has an influence, either good or bad. Every order we issue, be it written or oral, has an influence. I will deal in more detail a little later about our actions and orders and the considerations that govern them. Now, though, let's build further on the definition of leadership.

We've said that leadership is the art of influencing and directing. There are millions of men and women in leadership positions across America today issuing orders and giving directions to the people under them. But, do their actions and orders inspire their people? In all except the rarest of instances, the answer is NO. How about the actions of every boss or supervisor with whom you work? And what about you? You'll have to answer those questions.

Influencing and directing is leadership in action, and there is a right way that every great leader has found. Just any way won't suffice. It has to happen in *such as way as to obtain the respect, confidence, willing obedience, and loyal cooperation of the people under the leader's supervision.* Regardless of the position one holds, no person is a declared leader until their leadership has been ratified in the hearts and minds of all with whom they come in contact. You will hear supervisors in so-called "middle management" complain about not having sufficient authority, and you may say or think that yourself, but I say to you that if you have attained the respect, confidence, willing obedience, and loyal cooperation of your people, you will have all of the authority you'll ever need. A boss who has to depend upon the authority vested in the position he or she holds is a loser and unfit to hold the position they occupy. Thus, we define leadership as *the art of influencing and directing people in such a way as to obtain their respect, confidence, willing obedience, and loyal cooperation in order to achieve the goals, objectives, and purposes of the organization.*

I spent most of my adult life as an Army officer. It was an environment in which every officer was in constant competition with their peers for service school selection and promotion. Commanders were always aware of what an efficiency report rendered on an officer would do to his or her career, and so the ratings tended to be inflated. Commanders described over half of all officers in the Army as "outstanding," but the real facts are that, when comparing all officers in the Army to each other, half of them are "below average." Likewise, half of the supervisors at any level of business, industry, and the professions are below average. In fact, half the supervisors reading this concept are below average when comparing themselves to their peers. That's the bad news. The good news is that all of them and you can learn to be outstanding leaders of other people—starting today.

TRAITS OF A LEADER

First of all, you possess all of the necessary equipment. Each of you is endowed with certain personal qualities that, in the leadership business, we call the *Traits of a Leader*. The specific traits I'll mention are not the only ones that help to make up the human personality, but they are the ones that play the prominent role in leadership. The first of these is:

Bearing

The way we carry ourselves. A sloven-like carriage of one's body has a destructive influence. You've seen people with poor bearing and know what it does to their image. Some people use their bearing (synonymous with *presence*) to such an advantage that everything stops when they walk into a room. General George Patton understood that and used it to his great advantage. So did Generals George C. Marshall, Matthew B. Ridgway, and James Gavin. They prompted silence and stopped activity by simply appearing on the scene. No one I've known personally was as effective with his bearing as was Coach Paul "Bear" Bryant. Everything came to a halt and all eyes focused upon him when he entered a room. His reputation as a coach was a contributing factor but not the primary one. All of us have seen a few such leaders, but we have met thousands of others who never realized the real worth of their personal bearing.

Courage

Courage is of two kinds—physical and moral. Physical courage is the mental control of fear—not the absence of it. The more intelligent one is the more likely they are to be fearful of danger. In some respects, fear is one of our greatest friends, because it enables us to do super-human things. Every time I think of physical courage, my thoughts go back in history to Marshal Touraine who fought under Louis XIV. One morning, he was about to mount his horse to go and fight one of many battles in which he participated. A young aide, who had never missed a meal or heard a bullet fired in anger, saw Marshall Touraine's knees trembling, walked up to him, and with somewhat of a smirk said, "Marshall Touraine, I am astonished, sir, that a man of your stature and experience would let his knees tremble as he mounted his steed for battle." Marshall Touraine looked at the aide and said to him, "Young fellow, I'll admit that my knees do tremble, but if they knew where I would be taking them this day, they would tremble even more." That's the bottom line. The knees of both the coward and the courageous tremble, but the knees of the courageous warrior will always take him toward the enemy. I've known people who let a fear of flying keep them off of airplanes, and I've known Army officers who let fear affect their actions in combat. They had little, if any, respect among their peers.

The other kind of courage is *moral courage. It is the qual-*

ity that causes one to stand up for what is right regardless of the cost. It is not beyond the realm of possibility that it may cost you an opportunity for advancement, but the morally courageous leader cannot be bought and sold. Selfishness and egotism are close relatives and dominate the actions of the morally-bankrupt coward.

Initiative

Seeing what needs to be done and doing it without asking for permission or waiting to be told to do it. If it's in someone else's area or realm of responsibility, just get the right person involved in correcting it. I would never advocate breaking the line of authority, but I also would never advocate ignoring something, because it's not your responsibility. The great leader is constantly on the search for things that are right and things that are wrong. When the great leader sees things that are right, he or she immediately seeks out the person or persons who caused them to be right and rewards them in some appropriate way. When the great leader sees things that are wrong, he or she immediately seeks out the person or persons responsible and takes appropriate action to get the problem corrected, including such action as is necessary to see that there is no recurrence of it.

Enthusiasm

A sincere interest in the task at hand. Vocal volume is not indicative of sincere enthusiasm. The quietest person on the scene may be the most enthusiastic. He or she may just be wise enough to know that no one ever got chewed out for listening or made a major mistake for the same reason. *No one ever listened himself out of a job.* Neither have I ever heard of anybody being relieved of command in a military establishment for that reason. Enthusiasm is a sincere interest in the task at hand—that and nothing more.

Endurance

The indomitable spirit that drives one onward to unwavering perseverance, refusing to stop when the body says it can't continue, refusal to quit, refusal to fail, the constant expectation that eventually one will succeed. Some quit when the going gets tough or when they just don't feel good. Daylight saving time just causes some people to get tired an hour earlier, but no one ever gets tired on the day of a promotion or pay raise. Marathons are sometimes won by guts alone. The degree of one's physical endurance is often directly proportional to the degree of one's mental endurance. The midget can slay the giant if the midget either refuses to lose, or if the midget doesn't realize he's a midget in the first place. Coach Paul "Bear" Bryant was heard to say on many occasions that his teams prevailed on the gridiron, because those of his players with little or no talent never knew they didn't have it. Your commitment to endure against impossible odds will eventually put you in the lead, because the competition does not know the price you're willing to pay. An outweighed, lesser-talented, and lesser-experienced down-lineman on a football team, who is convinced that he will eventually beat his opponent on the other side of the line-of-scrimmage, may be beaten badly by his opponent in the first half. But we've all seen instances where mental endurance, guts, and perseverance made up for shortage of talent and physical skill. The lesser pulls even with the greater by the end of the third quarter and in the fourth quarter owns his opponent's soul. That's why football games are won and lost in the fourth quarter, and it's also the reasons why games of life are won and lost as well.

Decisiveness

The ability to make a decision and announce it with force and confidence—and without fear of its impact. I know a man who has been able to get by all of his life without making a tough decision. He makes a decision not to make a decision, because he fears the consequences. Somehow, though, he has succeeded in advancing to a high position, but rest assured, that somewhere along the way he will meet his Waterloo. Leaders may at a future time have to defend their decisions in a court of law, but such possible consequences will not sidetrack the decisive leader. A major part of decisiveness is stepping up to the line when the situation demands and making that tough decision that needs to be made.

Justice

The ability to deal fairly and equitably with all people, treating every person no differently than you would treat a member of your own family. Leaders who can't do that are unfit for the position they hold.

Judgment

The ability to reach a logical conclusion from a given number of facts bearing on a problem. A part of judgment is common sense, but every great leader knows there is nothing common about common sense. If you don't believe that, lay out the same facts to 10 or 15 of your associates whom you think to have good common sense and see how many of them reach the same conclusion.

Unselfishness

Putting the organization and others before one's self. Every truly inspirational leader of history appeared to own this trait in great abundance. A common thread running through all of these great leaders was an inner belief that they did not own themselves. To them, ownership belonged to God, their families, their country, their friends, and the cause they served. One of the greatest leaders you'll ever meet is my dear friend, Jerry Thomas, a former Vice President of HARCO Drugs whose inspirational leadership played a major role in helping to make HARCO one of the business success stories of our time. In less than a decade, HARCO parlayed one drug store into a company that sold to RiteAid for a figure approaching a half-billion dollars. *"Those who would walk over their own mother to reach the top will one day"*, Jerry once said, *"look around and find that their ladder of success is leaning up against the wrong building."* True enough, that ladder is unsound and like the house in Jesus' parable (Matthew 7:26–27, *The Holy Bible*), the ladder of the selfish is unevenly anchored upon the sand, and it's going to come crashing down—and great will be its fall. If you were the leader of an expedition to the North Pole in the winter time and find that you are one short of having enough arctic sleeping bags for your fellow explorers, I don't have to tell you who it is that goes without one. Rest assured, though, that they would never let you freeze, and at all other times in whatever the situation, they will take care of your needs in some way. Unselfish leaders find it second-nature to subjugate themselves to the people they lead. Unfortunately, we see all too many who don't fit that mold. As an old retired Army Sergeant Major (Jim Gallagher, one of the greatest soldiers to ever wear the uniform) said to me recently, "Instead of seeing our leaders of today applying the time-honored Three M's (Mission and Men before Me), I see all too much of Me, Me, and then Me." True enough, our society is replete with those who think the world owes them everything they need, regardless of whether they have earned it. Neither can they live peaceably without having things their way in the workplace and in their relationships with others, but the great leader will play the role of the unselfish servant always and every time.

Knowledge

Being well-read and learned in a wide range of matters. Knowledge enables you to talk intelligently with people from varied backgrounds, and a great knowledge of everything related to your profession also gives you a sixth sense about things. It's what some call *"feel,"* and there has never been a great leader who didn't have it. Sometimes, the leader has only a gut feeling about something, but invariably it turns out right for the great ones. You need knowledge that you might not think you need at the moment. About 35 years ago, an Army officer in command of a battalion had observed that almost none of the young Lieutenants fresh out of college could write effectively, and he knew they could never reach the fullness of their potential unless they could. He made a practice of interviewing each new officer, regardless of grade, and he asked each of them the same question to test their knowledge of English grammar. "I'm going to use a sentence," he would say, "and I want you to tell me how the word 'him' is used. Then, he would say, "I want him to go." If the officer couldn't tell him that "him" is the subject of the infinitive "to go" and that subjects of infinitives are in the objective case, that shell-shocked officer went to the English grammar class that the commander held at some place and time two hours each week for six months. He had only one officer to ever get the answer right but nailed him with a second question. He asked him, "Which is right: I don't mind him going or I don't mind his going?" The officer answered "him going," and bought himself a ticket to the class on English grammar. He didn't know that the possessive case of a noun or pronoun always precedes a participle phrase or a gerund. He attended the class along with all the others. They learned how to write, and they learned how to speak, and that commander still gets letters from many of those officers thanking him for it.

Tact

The ability to deal with others without offending them. It's been 45 years, but I remember a young second lieutenant at Fort Benning, Georgia, asking Captain Bill Weber, the only double amputee that the Army ever kept on active duty, to give him an example of a tactful and an untactful response to a given situation. Captain Weber answered him by saying, "Well, suppose you are looking into the face of a rather unattractive lady and tell her that her face would stop an 8-day clock. Now, that would be untactful stupidity. On the other hand, if you had said that when I look upon your face and into your eyes, time literally stands still, that would be tact." Now, one doesn't have to be in someone's presence to be tactful or untactful. You can do it with your public utterances. Almost every week, I read something in the newspaper about somebody having said something about somebody and then claiming that he was misquoted by a newspaper. It occurs to me that a person like that ought to have learned long ago that *no newspaper can misquote silence.* I read and listen to politicians and public officials who even go so far as to tell half-truths and even lie about each other. It seems to me that simply telling the truth about each other would be destructive enough. They end up damaging their own credibility and influence. So do the persons who fail to realize that the closer working relationships become the more tactful they must be. A father or a mother needs to be tactful even in their own home. Husbands should avoid actions and words that offend their wives, and wives should avoid offending their husbands. You can't be one thing at home and another thing outside the home.

Dependability

A quality that lets people know you can always be depended upon to keep your word, to be where you ought to be, and to always get the job done. It is evidenced by never letting your boss or your organization down and by keeping a commitment—always and every time. A part of dependability is to live by a cardinal principle of life that you will never let your boss make a mistake.

Integrity

The uprightness of moral principle, honesty in all things. Sadly, only a very few people are always honest in all they say and do. The problem with modern civilization is that we all too often mistake respectability for character. Respectability comes from doing what's right when people are looking. Character is doing the right thing when nobody is looking. I'll tell you this: You won't find very much traffic congestion on the straight and narrow road. While serving in Berlin during the building of the wall, I knew an Army officer who walked out of his office without locking his safe, which contained some secret and top secret documents. He got in his car and drove about half-way to his quarters and thought about what he had done—or hadn't done. He turned his car around, went back to his office, checked the documents and found none of them missing, locked his safe, signed the checklist, and immediately reported the security violation to his boss—knowing that it would end his military career. Here was a man of integrity. The Commanding General of Berlin at that time was Major General James Polk. He personally went to bat for that officer and saved his career, officially ruling that no compromise of classified material had occurred. A few years later, the officer I'm referring to took off with a buddy in a small airplane in Alaska, and they've never found them or the aircraft. He's buried somewhere, probably under a polar icecap, but he died holding the highest respect of those who knew him.

Loyalty

Allegiance and faithfulness—faithfulness up, faithfulness sideways, and faithfulness down. Either people just don't understand loyalty or else they just don't follow the rules. In case you haven't heard them, let me tell you what they are. The first rule is that no leader should ever speak disrespect-

fully to anyone else, on the job or off the job, about a boss
or a fellow supervisor. If you do that, you detract from that
person's effectiveness and consequently undermine your
own organization. Thus, you become disloyal to the very
organization that pays your salary and to which you have an
inherent responsibility to serve loyally. If you have any axes
to grind, have the guts to go rub nose-to-nose and eyeball-
to-eyeball with that person individually in private and tell
him or her the problem you have with them and why. But
don't make the grave mistake of sharing that conversation
with anyone else, particularly for the purpose of gaining
another's support for your side of an issue.

Secondly, if you ever observe a condition, become aware
of a policy, receive a directive, or whatever that you do not
believe to be in the best interest of the organization, you
must tell your immediate boss. You are disloyal to him or
her if you don't. Now, the way you tell the boss is a vital
part of loyalty. When you go to tell him or her, you do so
in one clear unbroken paragraph in language that a moron
can understand what it is you don't agree with and why—so
that no subsequent comment on your part is ever required.
Then, if the boss rules against you, you follow another rule
of loyalty. You support that directive or policy 110 percent.
All of those things you are in such agreement with that
you just can't wait to carry them out, you support only 100
percent. Every good boss in America is looking for special men and women whom they can rely upon to do that
very thing, but they are almost non-existent. There is, of
course, an exception to this rule. If something is against
the law, immoral, or against the dictates of your conscience,

you must refuse to carry out that order under any conditions—even if the boss continues to insist that you do. You
then must report it to somebody. The one thing you don't
do is to go back to your people and tell them that you don't
like what you're asking them to do, that you had gone to see
such and such and tried to get it changed. If you do that,
you have violated a principle of leadership that I will mention shortly. In fact, it is good policy to never divulge the
source of the orders you issue, unless a boss has asked you
to do so. Have the strength of character to issue orders and
instructions in your own name and then accept the responsibility for them. If you do that, there'll be no room in your
life to bad-mouth the organization that pays your salary.
If you insist upon the right to do that, then quit your job
immediately and do it to your heart's content—but the first
puff of strong wind that comes along is going to blow you
away, and you'll never know why.

Now, all of these 14 traits that I have defined exist to
some degree in all people, but they do not exist to the same
degree in any two people. Therefore, no two people have
identical personalities, and this means that all personalities
conflict. Herein rests an alleged dichotomy in leadership
doctrine, but no real dichotomy exists. Since all personalities conflict, such differences should have no impact on
senior-subordinate relationships. A so-called "personality conflict" cannot be used as an excuse for disloyalty or
failure to get along on the job, and failure to understand
that is tacit evidence of the lack of understanding of the
basic fundamentals of leadership. This doesn't mean that
anyone should always agree with the boss. In fact, when

two people on the job always agree, one of them is unnecessary. Yes-men are disloyal to the boss and disloyal to the organization, and keeping them around is the worse kind of feather-bedding.

So, all of the 14 traits exist to varying degrees in all people, and it is the degree of possession with which every leader must be concerned. It is incumbent upon you as the leader to make a continuous, honest-to-God, soul-searching self-evaluation of these 14 traits to determine those in which you believe yourself to be the strongest and let everything that you do reflect these qualities. This enables you to be consistent in the exercise of your leadership. We cannot be like anyone else. When we try it, we become phonies, and inconsistency is the result. We can't be wishy-washy—peaches and cream all week long and a tyrant on Friday or Saturday. All need to know what to expect of their leaders in the same way that children need to know what to expect of their parents. You can't dismiss a child from the table on Sunday for displaying the same bad table manners the child displayed all week long and got by with, all because you may have invited your church pastor over for dinner. The child won't understand it, and the people in the organization won't understand inconsistency either. So, we must always display our strong qualities while seeking to strengthen those in which we are weak. A weak quality may become a strong one if we work on it. That's why our self-evaluation must be continuous.

Earlier, I stated that no personality is more suited to leadership than another. Persons on opposite ends of the personality spectrum can be equally successful even in the same profession. No two people could be more different than Generals Omar Bradley and George Patton, but they were both successful, because they had the common sense to capitalize upon their dominant leadership traits.

In addition to one's personality traits, the leader has at his disposal some fundamental truths to guide him or her in the exercise of leadership. These truths we refer to as the *Principles of Leadership.* They are 11 in number and were derived from a study of both successful and unsuccessful leaders of history. Those leaders who were successful appeared to follow these principles. Those who failed as a leader appeared to violate them—either consciously, sub-consciously, or because they didn't know any better. The leadership principles keep the leader from making a mistake if he or she lets the principles guide his or her actions and orders. The first of these principles concerns the use of the Leadership Traits that I just finished discussing.

KNOW YOURSELF AND SEEK SELF-IMPROVEMENT. Knowing yourself means to conduct the soul-searching self-evaluation that I talked about earlier and then begin a conscious effort to improve upon your weak traits. To do this, it is important to accentuate the positive. We've already established that all of the traits exist to some degree in all people. So there is no such thing, for example, as total dishonesty. There is instead a certain degree of integrity, and it is the degree thereof that the leader must determine and seek to improve upon.

KNOW YOUR JOB AND ENOUGH ABOUT THE JOBS OF YOUR SUBORDINATES IN ORDER TO BE ABLE TO SUPERVISE THEM EFFECTIVELY: Not even a one-man business or undertaking is exempt from all of this principle. He or she does not have anyone to supervise, but they must know their job, and just learning the job may require supervision from some source. Regardless of the endeavor, knowing one's own job in addition to familiarity with the job of an immediate subordinate are vital requirements. Show me a Principal of a middle school who doesn't know when to use "I" and when to use "me" and doesn't know how to conjugate the verb "to be", or who doesn't know that the possessive form of a noun or pronoun always precedes a participle phrase or gerund, and I'll show you a middle school that is under-achieving in English grammar. Or, show me a high school principal who doesn't know how to factor an algebraic equation, doesn't know when to use reciprocals in solving algebraic problems, doesn't know how to balance a chemical equation, and who doesn't know how to calculate the volume of an irregular shaped rock, and I'll show you a high school that is under-achieving in math and science. A good school principal will know how his or her students are going to perform before national testing time.

MAKE DECISIONS IN A TIMELY MANNER AND ISSUE ANY IMPLEMENTING ORDERS IN SUFFICIENT TIME TO ENABLE YOUR PEOPLE TO REACT PROPERLY. Don't expect things to be done yesterday if you didn't think about them yourself until now. Reaction time must always be greater than the time it takes a leader to make a decision and put out the word. Required reaction time and deadlines must be keyed to the responding ability of the weakest links in the organization, and a good leader will know where those weakest links exist at any one moment in time.

SEEK RESPONSIBILITY AND TAKE RESPONSIBILITY FOR YOUR ACTIONS. Never make the mistake of blaming a subordinate in front of your boss when you have been called before the carpet because something wasn't done. Any time you're admonished for something that wasn't done or done poorly, you have already violated a leadership principle that I'll discuss in a moment. Prove that you can handle additional responsibility by accepting the responsibility that's already yours. Remember always that responsibility can never be delegated. Authority can but responsibility can't. As the sign on Harry Truman's desk read, "The buck stops here."

ENSURE THAT THE TASK IS UNDERSTOOD, SUPERVISED, AND ACCOMPLISHED. If this principle is observed, no one will ever have to answer to the boss because something wasn't done or because a standard isn't met. The main thing to remember is that it is not enough to simply issue an order or directive. We must ensure that it is understood and that its execution is supervised until it is completed. Earlier on, I spoke of the consequences of a lack of adequate knowledge on the part of a high school principal. Taking that a step higher, the Dean of one of the colleges in any of our major comprehensive research universities almost never walks into the classroom of one of his professors when a class is in progress. In the name of academic freedom and professional trust, the professor is left to go about his or her work with little or no supervision. The task of evaluating is left to the students, who are in no position to render a judgment. The assertion here is that an utter disregard of this leadership principle is costing America in terms of the quality of the students being graduated from the nation's institutions of higher learning. The result is a work force less prepared to turn the wheels of business and industry, and that is only one example. The fundamental truth is established here that a failure to be guided by this principle will cost the leader of any human endeavor, large or small, in some significant way.

SET THE EXAMPLE. The leader must set a personal standard of conduct that is higher than anything he or she expects from anyone else under his or her supervision. No one with less than impeccable moral character can gain and hold the respect of a subordinate with a higher moral fiber, and no leader can enforce a standard that they have not achieved personally. Also, while I'm talking about setting an example, let me caution you to watch your language. God's last name is not "Damn," and saying that it is causes you to lose the respect of those under you who know that it isn't. If you hear something that you think to be B.S., don't call it by those two four-letter words. Just respond by saying, "That's incredible." Now, if something is so incredible that you just have to call it something worse than incredible, just say that "It sounds like Bovine Scatology to me." Bovine Scatology means the same thing, and it is abbreviated the same way. All you've done is to elevate it to a higher level of academic excellence. In all seriousness, your example should be accompanied by a personal commitment that you will leave a pair of shoes too large for anyone who takes on your job when you're promoted upward. More importantly, your daily walk must be such that no person in the organization is given an iota of a reason to believe that he or she owns a higher moral character.

Know your people and look out for their welfare. If a leader does not know his or her people, he or she cannot possibly know their effectiveness or the specific training they require. We should do as much for those under us as we possibly can by honest means, but the best way to take care of the welfare of people is to give them the best training imaginable. Every person, regardless of sex, creed, race, or whatever has a right to be able to advance to the level of their incompetence, but they can't do that without training. One of a leader's mandatory duties is to develop other leaders, including being a mentor to his or her immediate subordinates. If you train them well, the job will get done while you're away from the organization. While in combat, I sought to remind myself daily that if that bullet with my name on it should come my way the men I loved and died for would have someone to lead them.

Keep your people informed. The only way an organization can function properly or be able to operate in the absence of the boss is to be completely informed. Ask yourself constantly what your people may not know and then make sure the information gets to them. During the Korean War, an Infantry battalion commander decided one night to send a section of tanks to reinforce an outpost about 500 yards in front of his main defensive line. It was a good action, because Chinese tanks had been heard in the area, and the men on the outpost were quite apprehensive. The problem was that the battalion commander didn't inform the outpost that he was sending the tanks out there.

In short, the company on the outpost thought they were Chinese tanks and took them under fire. The section leader of the tanks thought they were being fired upon by the Chinese, and returned the fire. Several men were wounded before the firing could be stopped, all because the battalion commander failed to let a leadership principle guide his actions. Fortunately, most violations occur in circumstances where life and death are not involved. No organization, however, escapes the impact of repeated violations of this important principle.

DEVELOP A SENSE OF RESPONSIBILITY AMONG SUBORDINATES. There are many things that a leader can do to help develop a sense of responsibility among his subordinate leaders. To the contrary, the most common way this principle is violated is to stand over people while they do their jobs and dictate exactly how the tasks are to be performed. There are numerous ways to skin a cat, and the best thing a leader can do is delegate authority to their subordinates and let them do the job their way. If the job is getting done, a smart leader will praise the person doing it and let him continue. Delegation of authority is meaningless unless it connotes freedom to make a mistake here and there. Now, there is a limit to how many mistakes a subordinate leader can be permitted to make. You can't quite live with a person who never makes the same mistake twice but makes every mistake once. Remember again that the leader can delegate authority but not responsibility. Delegating authority never relieves the boss of his overall responsibility. This bothers a lot of executive leaders—particularly those who fear the consequences of decisions being made.

TRAIN YOUR PEOPLE AS A TEAM. Wherever two or more people exist in an organization, effective teamwork is required. In small organizations, the existence of good teamwork, or the lack of it, is readily apparent, but as organizations become larger, effective teamwork among the organization's component parts all too often falls victim to the bureaucratic tendencies that the executive leadership permits to exist. One of the things that I observed when I took a job as a university administrator following retirement from the Army was that the division heads and their immediate subordinates tended to give first priority to their own staff responsibilities. Although it was their duty to act expeditiously on matters being staffed with them by other divisions, such action went lacking until their own staff functions had been accomplished. It took time, but we learned that effective teamwork could only exist by giving first priority to the staff actions of persons outside of our own divisions. Poor teamwork bordering on paralysis exists in any organization wherein any component part must wait on the actions of others. At the same time, we must never get so fixed in any routine or way of doing that we cease to look at other ways, other tactics, and other strategies. We need to not only be looking at things we do and ask why, but we need also to be looking at things that never were and ask why not. The end result we seek is an organization that is finely-tuned and working together in perfect harmony.

UTILIZE YOUR PEOPLE IN ACCORDANCE WITH THEIR CAPABILITIES. It's rare when you find a person who can do everything and do it well. There are those who can orchestrate, command, and preside over other leaders, and there are those who can perform well as a leader and teacher at one level but fail at another. We have all seen the excellent assistant coach who couldn't make it as a head coach. In the military profession, we see those who can command and others who are better suited to perform as professional staff officers. The wise leader will find out what his or her people can do and use them in that capacity. One of the most outstanding young officers in the Korean War was Captain Lewis L. "Lew" Millett. He was an artilleryman assigned as a forward observer with Company E of the 27th Infantry Regiment (The Wolfhounds). He took command of the company on the night of 27 November 1950 in an action when all of the officers in the company were killed including the Company Commander (Captain Reginald B. Desiderio who was awarded the Medal of Honor posthumously for his actions). Millett was able to hold the position against repeated Chinese attacks. He became an Infantryman the next day and subsequently led the two most famous bayonet charges in our Army's history. He received the Medal of Honor for his actions during one of those charges. It is the only instance in which succeeding company commanders received the Medal of Honor. As an artillery forward observer, he was not being used where he should have been. This principle of leadership is not followed very well in either the military or civil life, primarily because the leader doesn't take the time to find out what their people can really do and then take advantage of that knowledge and ability. Where no such position exists in an organization, the great leader will help that person to find a job that will enable him or her to realize the fullness of their potential.

The leader needs to remember that the 11 *Principles of Leadership* are guides—not laws. A leader may every now and then find a good reason for violating one or more of them, but they should be aware that they are doing so at the time and have a good reason why. The wise leader accepts the principles as fundamental truths to guide him or her in the proper exercise of leadership. Following them may not solve all of a leader's problems. It may require a lot of actions and orders to do that, but the leader can always be assured that being guided by the Leadership Principles will always ensure that his/her actions and orders will always have a positive influence on the people under their direction.

The leader of any organization has two basic responsibilities: ACCOMPLISHMENT OF THE MISSION AND THE WELFARE OF THE PEOPLE IN THE ORGANIZATION. These responsibilities are never really in conflict, but sometimes they may appear to be. This is the reason that General George Patton always stressed that "Your mission comes first—always and every time. Your people come next—always and every time. And you come last—always and every time." In actuality, each of the two responsibilities complements each other. If you don't look out for the welfare of your people, such failure will impact adversely on the overall effort of the organization. Again using a military example, an infantry company had been on the move during the Korean War for over two days without any sleep and had just completed a counterattack to restore a portion of Line Wyoming near the 38th Parallel. The time was about 2130 hours (9:30

p.m.), and the company mission was to dig in and prepare for a possible Chinese counterattack. The First Sergeant of the company had seen combat in Europe during World War II and was a highly respected noncommissioned officer. The company commander was a First Lieutenant with less than two years of service. Seeing how begrimed, tired, and weary the men were, the First Sergeant recommended to the company commander that three fourths of the men be allowed to get some sleep, keep one-fourth awake, rotate off and on during the night, and begin digging in the following morning. This was a tired man talking to a tired man. So, the company commander agreed. To make a long story short, the company was subjected to a tremendous Chinese artillery and mortar attack about 2:00 A.M. that night. When the attack began, the men of that company had plenty of energy, but it was too late to use it. The company commander and the First Sergeant thought they were looking out for the welfare of their men, but in failing to do what the mission required, they gambled with the lives of their people. The responsibility rested on the shoulders of the company commander, and the blood of his men will always be on his hands. Accomplishing the mission almost always takes care of the welfare of one's people, even though your people may not realize it at the time. It is worth restating that the accomplishment of the mission and the welfare of those under your supervision are never in conflict. At a moment in time, they may appear to be—but only in the mind of the leader. An objective analysis at another place and time will forever result in one conclusion: Accomplishing the mission would have taken care of the welfare of one's people.

The leader does not have to be a psychologist, but he/she must have knowledge of human behavior. The behavioral scientists tell us that all behavior, both good and bad, emanates from a desire to satisfy certain basic human needs. These needs are both physical and learned. The physical needs are food, shelter, clothing, and bodily activity. The learned needs are recognition, security, and social acceptance.

Almost everyone has heard of Maslow's Hierarchy of Needs. I won't qualm with what he says, but the problem with his theory is that a leader never knows where a person under his or her leadership is located in the hierarchy. So, Maslow's theory has little, if any, utility. The bottom line is that the leader must create an environment that enables the individuals under his or her leadership to satisfy their needs.

A knowledge of human behavior is one of the most powerful weapons in the leader's arsenal, and the good ones use it daily. Wherever these needs are ignored, the leader is failing to take care of the welfare of his/her people. Sadly, we've all seen that happen. No leader at any level will ever get the most from his/her people without applying knowledge of human behavior daily. Remember this: If a subordinate leader or an employee is not being required to perform outstandingly so that he or she can be recognized for it, the leader is failing that person. Again, I emphasize that the leader who cares for his/her people will provide them with the best training imaginable. It is only through training that a person can advance to a higher position in the organization. Even a foreman on an assembly line can train his people by sharing his knowledge with his workers during a lunch break.

Almost every boss in America makes a grave error by assuming that the pay scale takes care of the physical needs of his/her people, and as long as the organization is functioning and the business surviving, things are viewed as hunkydory. But, they almost always aren't. For example, if the students on a college campus aren't convinced that they are eating in the best cafeteria on any college campus in America, the President of that university is dropping the ball with reference to their need. The same is true of any other organization operating a dining facility. College campuses may have modern, well-equipped dormitories, but that doesn't mean that a university president has met his or her responsibility. Unless the student lives in safety in a dormitory free of drugs, alcohol, and is less than immaculately clean and well-maintained and where study conditions are less than ideal, the President is failing his students miserably. Buildings don't have to be new, but they do have to clean and well maintained. Someone is failing a student who is forced to live with a roommate who practices poor hygiene or does other things that have an adverse impact on a student's college life. If a laundry service is provided students in a dormitory, and students can't depend on their clothes being picked up at a scheduled time, properly cleaned, and returned on schedule, someone is failing those students. Unless someone is paying attention to students' needs for exercise and adequate rest and sees to it that they get it, even though they may be 18 years old and over, those students' needs are not being met. The end result is a college graduate less-prepared to perform outstandingly in the world that awaits him.

It is the mental and emotional aspects of the physical needs of one's people with which the leader should be most concerned. There aren't a whole lot of people in America who don't have a roof over their head, food to eat, and clothes to wear. Some Americans live well, and others don't live so well. All know that, but almost no leaders of the nation's large corporations know anything about their workers except their pay scales, and the result impacts far more adversely on their organizations than they realize. It's the quality of things, not whether something exists or not, that should most concern the leader. And remember this; it is not what you, the leader, think of the quality that counts. It's what your people think.

The learned needs of one's people are even more important to the leader than are the physical needs. Abraham Maslow wouldn't agree with that statement were he still alive, but I confess to believing it. The drive of the individual to satisfy one's learned needs is often so powerful that one will deny himself or herself food, physical comfort, and even subject themselves to great danger just to receive recognition, social acceptance, and a feeling of security or belonging. The smart leader knows this and establishes conditions and policies where such satisfaction is available. The astute leader is, however, careful that good recognition, for example, is not bestowed for mediocre performance. He or she is also careful to avoid excessive action. One of the leadership principles requires that the leader train and develop subordinate leaders who can stand on their own two feet without depending on others. Again, the leader must remember that <u>all behavior, both good and bad, stems from an effort to satisfy the basic human needs</u>. Herein rests the key to inspirational leadership and a strong argument that all mentally-balanced persons can be led by the great leader.

It would be a mistake in talking about a leader's two basic responsibilities, human behavior, and the leadership principles if I failed to mention the powerful impact a leader can have by applying what I like to call *Personal Touch*. Suppose that the President of General Motors is making an informal visit to his Cadillac plant in Detroit. Upon arrival, he goes into the Personnel Office, asks for the picture, name, and personnel data on one of the workers on the assembly line—just any worker. He just wants to be able to recognize him on sight, know where to find him, and what the worker does. He also finds out the worker's wife's name and his children's names and ages. As he is walking down the assembly line with the plant leadership and comes to the place where the targeted employee works, the assembly line suddenly stops (something he has pre-arranged). He looks up and down the line, appearing to wonder why it stopped, but searching out the employee whom he will speak to personally. First though, he says to all, "While the line is stopped, let me just tell all of you how much we appreciate what you do for Cadillac and General Motors." Then, he faces the targeted employee and says, "Clarence, I know how hard it is for the wife and me, and

I know how hard it must be for you and Edna to get little Warren, Shirley, and Maxie up, push breakfast down their throats, get them dressed and off to school, and make it to work on time. We've only got a 15-year old at home, and it's hard enough for us." He looks to all of them, sticks up his thumb, and says, "General Motors appreciates you, and don't any of you forget it." As he turns and walks on down the assembly line, it begins to roll again. Clarence is flabbergasted, as is everybody else in hearing distance. Can you even imagine the depth of emotion and wonder that the worker named "Clarence" experienced at that moment and what it did to him, the others who witnessed it, and eventually everybody else on that assembly line at Cadillac? Clarence probably won't sleep well for awhile, lying awake at night and wondering how the President of General Motors could care enough to know him by name and the names of his wife and children. Clarence will never miss another day of work unless he's hospitalized, and it would be a big mistake for anyone to speak disrespectfully of the President of General Motors in hearing distance of Clarence and his fellow workers at Cadillac.

What I have done so far without actually saying so is to give you three of the four basic considerations that the leader should take into account when deciding upon a course of action. Actions and orders must exhibit the strong traits of the leader, be guided by the leadership principles, and aid in accomplishing one or both of the leader's two basic responsibilities: the accomplishment of the mission and the welfare of his or her people. There's one other requirement. The leader's actions and orders must be consistent with the situation. No two leadership situations are ever the same despite their similarities. For example, let's say that you have had to admonish a subordinate leader recently for being late for work. This morning, he commits the same act again, but the situation is a lot different, and your actions will be different. Therefore, no two identical actions can be taken to solve a leadership problem. Every situation must be evaluated, and the action decided upon must be consistent with the present situation. The lesson here is that we can learn from observing great leaders, but we cannot mimic everything they do or have done. If all four of the considerations are followed, the leader's actions and orders will have a positive impact on the organization. Again, it may take many actions to solve a problem entirely or get the job done completely, but if all considerations are followed, the action taken will at least contribute to the purpose for which the action is intended.

The boss must have a goal toward which every action is aimed. For every organization, that goal is maximum effectiveness, Other words may be used, but the ultimate goal is to reach a condition of excellence that will enable you to get the job done in the most effective way possible. The goal of a State Superintendent might be "National Supremacy in Education." The goal of a military leader might be "Maximum Combat Effectiveness." However it might be stated, the goal should be high enough that it may never be obtained to the ultimate degree, but it gives the organization a lofty purpose and sets all in the organization on a common path. We begin with an intermediate objective or standard that is obtainable through a dedicated effort. Once that standard is reached, we raise the standard; and once the new standard is reached, we raise it again. The great leader is never satisfied with the present standard of excellence.

Every day, the leader is evaluating four things that are used to measure the effectiveness of the organization as well as the quality of leadership he or she is exerting. The four intangibles are called the *Indications of Leadership,* and as the title implies, they are accurate indicators of the success or failure of the person in charge. They also measure the effectiveness of any organization in any human endeavor. The four indications are *Morale, Discipline, Esprit, and Proficiency.*

Morale is the state of mind of the individual. It is not to be confused with happiness, because some people may be happy at working against the purposes of the organization. Morale is measured in terms of the degree of pride that one has in the proper performance of his/her duties. Morale does not, therefore, fluctuate as often as most people think. A person who has great pride in his duty performance will perform assigned duties in the best possible manner, regardless of his state of mind—but such may not last indefinitely. Most assuredly, it won't last indefinitely in the presence of poor leadership.

Discipline is a state of mind of the individual that ensures prompt and willing obedience to orders and instructions and the initiation of appropriate action in the absence of orders. This means that discipline can only be achieved through training. The people in an organization must know what the appropriate action is. A boss who fails to teach his subordinate leaders every thing he knows about the organization and its functions is wasting human assets. There are those who seek to secure their own jobs by denying opportunities for their subordinates to demonstrate the fullness of their abilities and protecting themselves by denying employment to job applicants by describing them as "overqualified." That type of person is a loser and a bottleneck in any organization.

Esprit (or Esprit de Corps) is the deep-rooted pride and loyalty that members feel for their organization. It is measured in the military by staying power under stress and is evidenced by a mutual feeling between a leader and his men that they own a superior quality and capability—that they have an unbeatable combination. Esprit is built by pushing an organization to accomplish the near impossible—something of such difficulty that the people themselves thought to be far beyond their own abilities - and then bestowing high recognition upon them. Never make the mistake of praising an unworthy performance.

Proficiency is knowing how to get the job done and having the physical ability to do it. Having such knowledge and ability will not ensure that the mission of an organization will be accomplished. It takes all four of the Indications of Leadership working in concert. A high degree of Morale, Discipline, Esprit, and Proficiency are all required. They are interrelated and interdependent. Something that impacts adversely on one of them will eventually have an adverse impact on the others.

Every leadership problem can be identified as either a problem of Morale, Discipline, Esprit, Proficiency or a

GOD & COUNTRY FOREVER

combination thereof. Once a problem is identified, the next step is to determine the cause. The boss then decides upon a course of action to eliminate the cause, using the four considerations discussed earlier as guidelines. The bad leaders treat symptoms, and if you think back through all of your experiences, I think you'll conclude that most of your bosses did that very thing. They treated symptoms instead of getting to the heart of the problem. So, the smart leader will follow three steps in leadership problem-solving: *Recognize the problem. Determine the cause. Eliminate the cause.*

No leader will ever achieve a 100-percent level in any of the Indications of Leadership, but this is the lofty goal that every great leader strives to obtain. Finally, let me say this about the Indications of Leadership. You may have a lousy boss who may complicate your leadership problem and increase the challenge that you face, but never lay the blame for low Morale, Esprit, Discipline, and Proficiency on your boss. That's what the losers do. Where they don't exist to a high degree, lay the blame on the person you see in the mirror.

What I have discussed in this treatise is only the basic concept of leadership. It is the framework on which all elements of leadership are contained, and every leader can fit himself into that framework and function outstandingly as a leader of other people. If the leader goes outside that framework, he or she may succeed to some degree, but somewhere along the way they will make a serious mistake. In some professions and organizations, major mistakes can be made with little consequence, but in others, such as vital product manufacturing and the military profession, the

72

leader has no such leeway. If a business leader makes a mistake, the business may fail, but if the military leader fails in his role, the nation may fall. With the military commander, human life and the survival of the United States are at stake and in any other activity where the product or service is vital to America's survival; the leader is left with no leeway to err. All such comparisons notwithstanding, a leader in the military, business, industry, or the professions who fails to master the art of leading people is doing a disservice of some proportion to the United States of America.

The padding on "*The Concept of Leadership*" takes many more pages to apply. What I endeavored to do in this article is to lay the framework only. It will be up to you to apply the padding through personal study and effort, because sometime in the past, our nation's educators made a major blunder by failing to include Leadership Doctrine in the curriculum of our nation's colleges and universities. The relatively few students who enroll in ROTC courses on our college campuses receive some leadership training but nothing sufficient to prepare them for the tasks that lie ahead.

"*The Concept of Leadership*" applies equally to every organization in America—from a large multi-national organization to a local Waffle House. Rarely, however, do the bosses of those organizations realize it, and the end results are lower productivity, irresponsible behavior, disregard for the nation's laws, and ever-prevailing conflicts between management and labor. The shouted challenge is to build a stronger, safer, and better America, and the American Patriotism Association seeks to play the leading role in putting America on the right path to that new level of greatness.

Young leaders entering business, industry, and the professions cannot be expected to deal with problems successfully if they aren't being taught. Preparing American youth to lead successfully should begin in high school and be continued in college. Even if attempted, such an undertaking is doomed to failure unless the teacher is prepared to do it—and they aren't. In higher education, the better students in particular find themselves in leadership positions, but learning to lead is left to trial and error by the students themselves. Higher education is not only failing to equip its students to be outstanding leaders but is also failing miserably to prepare our young Americans for the cruel world that awaits them. The following article highlights a part of the problem.

A MESSAGE TO
HIGHER EDUCATION

REGARDLESS OF ASSERTIONS TO THE CONTRARY, higher education is failing to prepare its graduates to perform effectively in the cruel world that awaits them.

In the foregoing article on Leadership, the author alleged that the failure of College Deans and Department Heads to visit the classrooms of their professors and evaluate their teaching performance is costing America in terms of the quality of the students being graduated. This sacred hands-off policy, I assume, emanates from the insistence of the American Association of University Professors (AAUP) that evaluating and supervising a professor's classroom performance would be degrading and encroach upon the Holy Grail of academic freedom. Whatever motivates the practice, I stand behind the assertion I made.

If there is some inviolate policy that prevents Deans and Department Heads from visiting the classrooms of their professors on a regular basis, then an apology is perhaps due those who would supervise the performance of their professors if it were permitted. My experience, however, tells me that the whole of higher education is content with leaving the evaluation of professors to the students themselves. It is also my experience that Professor "Easy-A McVeigh" almost always receives a high rating from his students. College is not much of a challenge already, and professors like "Easy-A McVeigh" make it even less so.

There is a problem with the "Easy-A McVeigh's" and higher education in general. They fail to prepare most students to live and perform effectively in the world that awaits them. Except for the value that one might attach to the diploma itself, the cost of four years of college at the least expensive of institutions is a heavy price to pay for the real amount of preparation for life after college that the student receives. With a full academic load, the student will spend only 16 hours in the classroom each week and perhaps a couple of hours of lab work, assuming he or she does not cut a class. The other 150 hours in the week belong to the student. There's some homework to do and occasionally a paper to write, but the total time required of the average student is less than one would expect to spend at a part-time job.

The school year takes up nine months on the calendar, but included in it is a half-week off for Thanksgiving, two weeks off for Christmas, and a week for spring break. Then, in between class years, there's three months of down time during the summer with no academic requirement. With careful schedule planning to avoid Saturday classes and a little luck, a student can spend half of the days in a year off campus and never miss a class. Even more astonishing is the fact that the student spends only about 8.0 percent of the year's time in the classroom. Regardless of claims to the contrary, college life is not nearly the challenge that some profess it to be. In fact, anyone with average intelligence can get a college degree.

With the recessional thundering behind them in slow and stately rhythm, the graduating seniors, even those finishing summa cum laude and magna cum laude, will march from the college campus into a strange world with no real idea of what awaits them. Immediately, they find themselves in a dog-eat-dog environment where a 'C' won't give them a passing grade and where one can't get some answers wrong and still make an 'A'. A professor or two may have cautioned them along the way that there will be no more summer-long vacations and 16-hour work weeks, no spring breaks, that Christmas will be on 25 December, and Thanksgiving will come on a Thursday, but only the rarest of students get the message. What they really see is a professor who teaches 15 to 20 hours a week and for whatever reason is gone from his office a large part of the time.

If the student with a probing mind goes looking into their professors' backgrounds, he or she will discover the most troubling of things that characterize the faculty of every college and university across the land: *A significant percentage of the professors have never held a responsible position in the cruel and challenging world that they are supposedly preparing their students to enter.* Immediately upon acquiring their Baccalaureate Degree, significant numbers of professors entered graduate school, acquired a Masters Degree, taking advantage of every available stipend and fellowship available, and remained on the college scene until they acquired their Ph.D. The primary source of their knowledge and expertise is the written word, most of which comes from the pens of professors like themselves. If someone really wants to learn something, the very best source would be a person who has "been there and done that outstandingly," but professors with such qualifications on college campuses are an endangered species. Therein rests a monumental shortcoming in higher education, and the problem will continue until academia recognizes that an "Earned Doctorate" is not the most important qualification that a professor can possess.

Next to Godliness, Education would have to be ranked first among the things necessary to the survival of America and the way of life it represents. Education has a moral obligation to prepare every young American to realize the fullness of his or her potential. This can never happen, unless the best teachers are doing the teaching, and the best researchers are doing the research. Professors are expected to do both, and in more cases than not, they are weak at one or the other. Consequently, both teaching and research are adversely affected. Tutorship is practically non-existent, and the advising and counseling function, particularly at the large comprehensive research universities, borders on being a joke. The present practice of requiring professors to "publish or perish" is a joke and not a funny one. Demanding that all professors spend most of their time researching is a colossal waste of time, effort, and money and detracts from their teaching performance.

Wisdom would suggest that Higher Education should be divided into three segments: administrators, teachers, and researchers with each segment having no other function. Teachers would be able to teach more classes during the week, and researchers would be able to devote more hours to research. The quality of both teaching and research would undergo a quantum increase without increasing the number of faculty members.

There's an exception to most rules, and the assertion just made has one as well. It would be beneficial for university administrators, particularly presidents and vice presidents who are eminently qualified in an academic discipline, to teach a class during one semester of the academic year. Contact with the students would give the administrators a better appreciation of the quality of the student body and enable them to more adequately fulfill their responsibilities for determining the appropriate strategic direction of their respective institutions. If the foregoing changes were made, a higher level of excellence would result immediately.

Researchers should be selected according to their ability to conduct research in their areas of expertise. Professors should be selected according to their ability to teach, with practical experience being a major criterion for selection. Higher Education is unable to provide adequate evidence that an "earned doctorate" is half as reliable in predicting success of position applicants as is "demonstrated ability to do the job." If I needed a Professor of Writing and Journalism, I would go after a great writer like Rick Bragg without regard to any degrees the other applicants might hold. Yet, one will seldom see a list of qualifications for a professorial position that does not list an "Earned Doctorate" as a qualifying criterion, the reason being that faculty members without earned doctorates lower a university's national ranking, the quality of the professors on board notwithstanding.

Colleges and universities across the land are never hesitant in boasting about high graduation rates, particularly among athletes, but nothing is said about what the graduates know. In the foregoing article on Leadership, I spoke of a military commander who observed that his newly-commissioned officers coming directly out of college could neither speak nor write effectively. I admit to being that commander, and I can state without wincing that I would never have signed some of their diplomas. If college students can graduate without knowing how to write and speak effectively, how much have they really learned? "Leaving no one behind" is a worthy goal, but simply pulling a student along amounts to *working hard to achieve the low standards we set for ourselves.* A college degree should be a testimonial to a minimum level of acquired knowledge and skill. Sadly, that is not the case, and America will never realize the fullness of her potential until our colleges and universities across the land begin to prepare their students adequately to live, thrive in, and contribute to the business, industrial, and professional world that awaits them.

The whole of America recognizes that most of our colleges and universities have their priorities out of order— that practically all of the truly outstanding professors are underpaid and some coaches allegedly overpaid for what they are contributing to the betterment of the nation and mankind. True enough, some coaches are well-compensated—not just for being a winner but also for what they do to mold the lives of the young men and women under their watchful eye. The great ones serve as an inspiration to their players and instill in them some important qualities of life that they would never acquire any other place on campus. No price tag can be placed on this essential side of education.

At some of the nation's largest universities, the tenures of a lot of people, including the University President, rest exclusively upon the success of the football and basketball programs—not upon any academic standards that the university professes to embrace. This happens because failure to win is readily identifiable with losing, and Americans won't tolerate a loser. *Winning is the American way, and America's will-to-win and will-to-fight have made and kept us free. Our future survival will depend no less upon this vital spirit, and so it must be kept alive and passed to generations of Americans yet unborn.* I think it was Coach "Red" Blaik who had the following words of General-of-the-Army Douglas MacArthur inscribed prominently for his football players to read each time they entered the football stadium at West Point: *"On the fields of friendly strife are sown the seeds that upon other fields, on other days, will bear the fruits of victory."*

The will-to-win and the will-to-fight will play the key role in the longevity of the United States, provided Americans everywhere can be made to understand that winning and losing apply equally to athletics and academics. Winning a national championship in football, basketball, or baseball should be the goal of every institution of higher learning in America, but national supremacy in education is also a worthy goal with which everyone connected with these institutions should be completely obsessed. It takes great coaches and players to win national championships, and it will take great administrators, researchers, and teachers for an institution to achieve national supremacy in education. The attempt to acquire them, however, is a scanty and misguided undertaking on most campuses across the nation.

The large comprehensive research universities in particular have a tendency to spend excessively on buildings and facilities that have a minimal impact on academic achievement. Millions are spent on bricks and mortar that could be used to double, triple, or quadruple the salary scale of deans, department heads, and professors in order to attract more of the nation's heavyweights, *who have been there and done that.* Except for laboratory facilities and associated equipment, bricks and mortar have no impact on academics, but this simple truth is not penetrating the gray matter of the decision makers in higher education. The primary thrust seems forever aimed at building larger and more beautiful buildings and facilities with nicer and more expensive furnishings that administrators believe to be essential to furthering the image of the university, promoting viability, attracting blue chip athletes, and enrolling greater numbers of gifted students. All of these are worthy goals, but a bricks-and-mortar strategy will not attain them.

The shouted challenge is for someone somewhere to step forward, take on Godzilla, and lead in a concerted effort to harness the support of Americans everywhere—in and out of education, politics, and government–to cause our institutions of higher learning to get their priorities in order. It won't be easy, however, to get people excited about academics, because the average American sees no need for change. I drew that conclusion from a mini-poll I conducted recently among 10 adult men with an intent of determining how much interest they had in academics as compared to football. All 10 knew who coached the football team at Auburn University, but not one among them could name either of the institution's last three Presidents. I suppose that's the reason newspapers have a "Sports" section but give no thought to including a daily section on "Academics."

As far afield as it may appear, I can envision the reporting of daily news about "Academics" in the same way that newspapers cover sporting events. Almost every daily newspaper in America has a "Sports Section" that keeps America informed about everything going on in the world of sports, but few people, including those in the Education business, can tell you very much about what's happening on America's college campuses. Millions of Americans know that Joe Paterno coaches football at Penn State and that his Nittany Lions had a good season in 2005. Millions more know that the Texas Longhorns won the national football championship by beating the University of Southern California Trojans in the big game, but how much do these same Americans know about the academic achievements of these two large comprehensive research universities? The truth is that they know almost nothing about how well or how poorly these institutions are doing the things for which they exist. Every daily newspaper in America needs an "Academics Section" that informs the public of what is going on at X University, whose doing it, and how well. In the same way that the Sports Section covers the whole of America and the world, the Academics Section should do likewise.

Over a period of time, great interest would come to be generated about news items that reflect unfavorably on a professor, student body, or an institution of learning. Athletic coaches and teams are brought to judgment by daily reporting of their every action. Such scrutiny, publicity, and pressure act collectively and in concert to improve the overall performance of the coach and the team. The same type of daily scrutiny, publicity, and pressure can be brought to bear on the staff, faculty, and student body at every academic level across our land. The result would be a more educated America, and that alone would be worth far more than the cost of hiring enough probing reporters and correspondents to fill an "Academics Section" of the local daily paper.

There's another inequity on campus involving athletics and academics that needs to be addressed. Generally speaking, there are two categories of students on a college campus—the student-athletes and all-the-rest. From the student athlete's perspective, he or she faces the greatest challenge and pays the greatest price. The athlete carries a full academic load and spends more time practicing his or her sport than the average student spends in the classroom. For the elite athletes, the additional time and effort can pay off in the form of multimillion dollar professional contracts. However, there is no bonanza awaiting the other students on campus regardless of their talents and academic achievements. A case can thus be made that student athletes enjoy the best of both worlds—that they are in a win-win situation. But a closer look leads to an altogether different conclusion.

Only a very small percentage of the student athletes make it to the professional ranks, and no gigantic signing bonus or lucrative contract awaits them. At the end of their senior year, they enter the same dog-eat-dog world as all other graduates, having spent four years of preparation with less study time available to them than was afforded other students. Favors and other acts of assistance from alumni and others were available to their non-athlete counterparts, but no favors of any sort and kind could be accepted by the student athlete. A bank loan, bus or plane ride, gift, and a myriad of other favors are available to other students, but let it be reported that a student athlete had received such support from some coach, alumnus, or avid supporter, and both the university and the student athlete are in great trouble with the NCAA. Ergo, the ground is not level for athletes and other students on campus.

The inequities between athletes and other students have prompted recommendations by some that student athletes should be paid for playing a sport that people pay to see. On the large campuses in particular, ticket sales, individual and corporate gifts to the athletic program, monies from radio and television, and monetary benefits obtained from businesses that market items bearing school logos bring millions to the institution. The student athlete and the game he or she plays are the attraction and the catalyst that turn on this free-flowing money spigot, and those who say that the student athlete should share in the bounty make a case compelling enough to at least convince higher education to remove the inequities between the student athlete and every other student on campus. If this were made to happen, university presidents and athletic directors could devote more time to the primary purposes for which they exist.

It is interesting that of all people in our society only the student athlete on a college campus is deprived of the rights and privileges afforded every other American citizen—except those being judiciously punished by a court of law. Certain rights and freedoms afforded to Americans have been taken from the student athlete by Higher Education in an attempt to level the ground for athletic recruitment among the nation's colleges and universities. It works to a degree, but it's difficult to accept the adage that the same result could not be obtained by the enactment and enforcement of a set of laws that punish the offender and not the student athlete. The amount of time, effort, and money spent by the nation's colleges and universities in the name of "institutional control" impacts adversely on the primary role of Higher Education and should be adequate motivation to seek a way to return matters of law and order to the Executive, Judicial, and Legislative Branches of government. *Higher Education's role is teaching, research, and service—not enactment, interpretation, and enforcement of the law.*

Finally, before closing the book on Higher Education, there's something that needs to be said about a thing called *"tenure"* that new professors pursue with reckless abandon. The desire to acquire it is a powerful motivator until it is attained. Once granted, however, it is no longer an incentive and does nothing to improve performance or professionalism. It provides an incredible degree of job security that only a felony or act of moral turpitude can endanger. In my view, *tenure* stagnates a university and makes it most difficult to improve faculty quality by a judicious application of removal and replacement. On balance, the granting of tenure does more harm than good, and Higher Education would do well to give it an honorable burial without delay—and thereafter attempt no postmortems or resurrections.

Hopefully, Boards of Trustees, Chancellors of University Systems, and University Presidents across the land can be persuaded to take a serious look at the inequities, problems, and misaligned priorities mentioned in this dissertation and act accordingly. A pipedream? Sadly, the answer is most likely YES, but what a wonderful undertaking it would be!

In addition to the regular students and student athletes on campus, there is another category of young men and women on the campuses of about 250 of the nation's institutions of higher learning who are preparing themselves for the noble task of keeping America free and safe for their fellow students and for Americans in all walks of life. Most of them didn't know what they were getting themselves into when they elected to take this course of study. The students I'm talking about are those enrolled in either Army, Navy, or Air Force

ROTC and constitute the institution's corps of cadets. Persuading college freshmen to test the waters and over the next four years transform them into confident young leaders prepared to take on the awesome responsibility of leading soldiers in battle is one of the most challenging and soul-satisfying experiences a military leader will ever know. It goes without saying that the first milestone is to get them on board, and that is what the substance of the following article is all about. The curricula of the Army, Navy, and Air Force programs vary substantially, but the method of successful enrollment is the same.

Though challenging and difficult, there is a way to succeed in the effort. Inasmuch as the ROTC program is completely essential to the nation's security, I have elected to include in this book a methodology for a successful enrollment effort on any college campus.

MILITARY TRAINING ON THE COLLEGE CAMPUS

One may dislike the presence of the military uniform on a civilian college campus, but the common good of the republic is best served by a military officer corps in which significant numbers have been exposed to the liberality associated with the nation's civilian institutions of higher learning . . .

EXCEPT FOR THE PARENTS OF ROTC SCHOLAR-ship recipients, it is rare indeed for fathers and mothers to send a young boy or girl off to college expecting them to don a military uniform and pursue a course of study in Military Science. With exception of the service academies and military schools, Military Science exists only as an elective and not one of the mandatory courses leading to a degree in any academic major. Consequently, significant numbers of students enrolling in Military Science (another name for ROTC) is something that happens only through a sustained, deliberate, and overt effort on the part of the Professor of Military Science (PMS). Despite how unattractive the military uniform might be on a college campus, there is a way to overcome any and all obstacles to enrollment confronting the PMS. Having served as PMS at the University of Alabama from 1974 to 1978, I have elected to include in this book a formula that proved to be successful at a time when other colleges and universities were experiencing difficulty. My reason for including the subject in this book emanates from my deep conviction that successful Military Science programs on college campuses are essential to building a stronger, safer, and better America.

The military uniform wasn't very popular on the college campuses across America from 1968 to 1978. The anti-military sentiment that gripped the nation following the 1968 Tet Offensive in Vietnam had taken its toll on college ROTC enrollment, and the Armed Services struggled to meet their need for commissioned officers. The problem had been further compounded by the cessation of the draft in 1974, when large numbers of students enrolled in ROTC to avoid the draft suddenly disappeared. As a result, the Army in particular faced a manpower crisis in its junior officer ranks.

By the summer of 1974, ROTC enrollment at the University of Alabama had dropped to under 150. One of the buildings used by the Army ROTC had been burned and a demonstration conducted against the ROTC Program by massive numbers of the staff, faculty, and student body. The military uniform was not a welcome sight on the University of Alabama campus when the Army sent me there in 1974, but over the next four years we were able to increase the number of cadets by over 2,000. For such use as other Professors of Military Science may find appropriate, the following is a capsule of how the enrollment effort was fashioned and orchestrated.

It is nearly impossible for a Military Science program to gain acceptance and popularity among the faculty and student body on a civilian college campus. Liberalism and anti-military sentiment generally run rampant, and the challenge to become the most popular activity on campus is so great that most Professors of Military Science become victims of the challenge itself. Defeatism and futility dominate their attitude and doom the enrollment effort at the outset. Success demands the opposite, and failure is inevitable if a PMS either doubts his ability to succeed or permits such an attitude to exist among his assistant professors.

In the Army, one often hears the expression that "I'm not running a popularity contest," and it is entirely true that no good commander ever does. However, a college campus is far removed from the Army, and if a Professor of Military Science is to overcome anti-military sentiment or general disinterest in the ROTC program by the university faculty and student body, the PMS must run a popularity contest of a sort through hard work, calculated action, mixing with students, passing out kudos, sharing academic interests, conducting a guidance and counseling program, and being the best and most helpful friend the student body has on campus. In short, he must have lofty goals that he is obsessed with reaching—come what may. He must decide at the outset what price he is willing to pay, how hard he is willing to work, how deeply he is willing to become involved in every activity on campus where students are located—and how much support and cooperation he will require from the University Staff and Faculty.

The first thing a PMS must do is to review the entire thrust of the ROTC program and structure it in such a way as to harmonize the objectives of the Army with the goals of higher education. While most Professors of Military Science would assert that their programs are in harmony with higher education, my personal experiences tell me that most are not. Only when the Administration, Faculty, and Student Body can readily see that the Military Science Program meets a pressing need will the program gain the necessary support and enthusiasm from every segment of the university.

The following key elements are mandatory if "milidemic harmony" is to exist ("Milidemic" is a word I coined in 1974 to describe the relationship between academia and those wearing the uniform on a college campus). Attainment of such harmony depends upon the establishment of academic credibility and acceptance by a university's staff and faculty of the need for a strong Military Science curriculum on campus. This requires that the purpose of the ROTC program be spelled out and disseminated to every segment of the University, the most effective way being to do it on a piecemeal basis and almost always indirectly as a part of some other communication. Words must be selected and pieced together in such a way as to be academic or at least carry an academic tone. The totality of the stated purpose must relate directly to the aspirations of the university and the student body. This means that the PMS must stress those aspects of the Military Science program that benefit the institution and society. The following objectives were espoused at the University of Alabama in 1974—1978, and they alone aided the enrollment effort:

> *The Military Science program is designed to aid the student in developing those habits and attitudes which will make of him or her a better student and increase his or her chances of graduating with a better education and higher academic achievement.*
>
> *The Military Science program provides the student an opportunity to learn and practice the art of leading people. Recognizing that there is a great difference in cognition and volition, the program has been structured to give the student actual practical experience in leading people and managing resources—training designed to prepare the student to reach the pinnacle of his or her chosen profession.*
>
> *The Military Science program enables the student to learn about the military profession and the role it plays in our democratic system of government. The freshmen and sophomore courses enable such knowledge to be acquired on the campus without having to serve in the Armed Forces.*
>
> *The Military Science electives enrich the student's course of study and count toward his or her graduation requirements. Taking these courses also opens up an additional career option to the student, enabling him or her to gain a commission and serve in the Army as an officer, or serve in the Reserves or National Guard while pursuing another chosen career.*
>
> *Military Science provides the student membership in*

*a close-knit fraternal organization where social acceptance
is assured.*

*Military Science programs on college campuses is the nation's
way of ensuring that all of the influences of higher education are transported into the Armed Services—a mandatory
requirement in a democracy.* This one stated purpose should
be emphasized on campus more than any other, as it is key
to the degree of the program's support among the Staff and
Faculty.

The problem of getting the message across that higher
education must play a key role in the nation's security
through the teaching of obligatory citizenship and responsible observance of the First Amendment is the greatest
challenge the PMS will face. This is an inherent role of the
PMS, but few recognize that such is so, and even fewer
know how to cope with it. If the ROTC program is to realize
its full potential, this message must come through, and the
PMS just might well find that the vacuum created by seg-
mented curricula in the various academic disciplines must
be filled through the ROTC program. If the PMS doesn't
do it, it won't get done. Had the problem been dealt with
sufficiently in years gone by, the acts of millions during the
unpopular war in Vietnam would have taken on a different character. Unquestionably, millions of Americans in the
late 1960s and early 1970s proved themselves to be totally
ignorant of our own system of government and every
American's responsibility to it.

The present generation of Americans must have no misgivings as to the subservient role of the military forces and

be clearly shown that the survival of the republic depends upon an understanding of its working parts and the unshakable support of the system during times of war—even those in which the nation's actions take an unpopular turn. Every cadet must hear this message repeatedly in the classroom, and the PMS needs to send memorandums to the most well-known and respected members of the faculty asking how higher education can best educate America on responsible citizenship and the role of the military in our system of government. The memorandum should state that *key figures in higher education, influential politicians, and millions of other Americans, both young and old, from all walks of life attempted to cause the military forces to rebel against the duly-elected civilian authority and quit the war in Vietnam—an act extending far beyond the reaches of the First Amendment.* Out of a combination of ignorance of our government's working parts and the absence of forethought of the grave consequences involved, many sought unwittingly to have the Armed Forces participate in the destruction of our democratic form of government by bestowing more power on the military establishment than it can have in a democracy or even in a Communist dictatorship. Dissent against the nation's actions and policies should be directed against the elected civilian officials of government and not against one of its subservient institutions. Arrogant displays of military power in the absence of civilian direction are not characteristic of a democracy.

Even if every faculty member fails to respond, the PMS has sent his message, and the total impact of such memorandums written by Professors of Military Science at 250-

plus institutions of higher learning across the nation would be monumental. Indeed, many may come to appreciate that the Officer Corps of the Uniformed Services knew, understood, and held fast to their oaths of office and in so doing formed the cement that held the nation together during the greatest test of our democratic form of government in the history of the republic.

When wars begin, all Americans everywhere must decide whether the preservation of our democracy outweighs any disagreement over the war or the danger to their own lives. It is a choice that can't be evaded, and the American people have to be taught enough to realize that the choice exists and of the grave consequences of selecting the wrong course of action. This is a major task of higher education, and it cannot be restricted to a Political Science Curriculum or a school of law. But, one won't find it in any professor's lesson plan on any campus anywhere, and so the initiative must come from the Professor of Military Science. If done with the utmost of courtesy and tact, its effect will be to neutralize anti-military sentiment among the university staff, faculty, and student body.

A thorough understanding of the role of the Armed Forces in our system of government is so vital to the nation's survival that the whole matter will be mentioned more than once in this book. There cannot be a stronger, safer, and better America unless every segment of our society understands our own governmental structure and its working parts and loyally supports its policies and procedures—both those enumerated and the ones unstated but inferred.

During my last two years as Professor of Military

Science, the Army sent me to explore a large number of ROTC programs across the nation. The one shortcoming I noted more than any others was the general feeling by most educators that the Military Science program had limited academic value. In almost every instance, only one credit hour was being awarded for freshman courses. The reason given by university administrators was the same in every instance—lack of sufficient academic worth to merit the normal three hours of credit given for other electives on campus.

Whether right or wrong, valid or invalid, justified or not justified, over-emphasis on purely military skill type training conflicts with the goals of higher education, and there is a limit beyond which the PMS should not proceed. Training which will be received and assimilated during summer camp should be minimized on campus. Those things that have an equal or near equal application in the civilian world should be that which receives the most emphasis and visibility. Leadership theory and application, management, democracy, vital and national interests of the United States (taught with care and caution), public speaking, map reading, military history, confidence building activities, tutoring, and advising and counseling need the most emphasis. These give the program academic credibility and complement the university's academic goals. Dismounted drill, weapons training, tactics, logistics, military justice, and Army administrative procedures need to be included, but they cannot be permitted to dominate the program. The student must gain the perception that what he is being taught is at least as valuable as that being received in his major course of study and that he or she is acquiring useful knowledge that is not available anywhere else on campus. When this occurs, "milidemic harmony" between the institution and the ROTC program becomes a reality. This happened at the University of Alabama, and the number of credit hours for the basic ROTC courses was increased and resulted in even greater numbers of students enrolling in Military Science.

Professors of Military Science can benefit greatly from the very nature of higher education. Institutions of higher learning were initially formed to "search for truth." The purpose of their origin was therefore research. The teaching function was an added responsibility that came along later, and it may come as a surprise to many that the two roles have not lost their priority. As I alluded to earlier in "A Message to Higher Education," research and professorial preoccupation with "publish or perish" remain the driving forces. In recent years, the large institutions in particular have taken on an additional responsibility—that of being expected to provide solutions to the nation's problems. While all three of these roles are related, they often come in conflict. To be sure, they compete for the time of both the university administration and the faculty. Consequently, the faculty's priorities change and the student is the one to suffer most. Students are made to feel that they are intruding on a professor by simply walking into his or her office, though they may have made an appointment. While this is a troubling reality, it works to the advantage of the PMS and his assistant professors. By gaining enough knowledge of the various majors and disciplines, the PMS finds himself in a position to fill a vacuum in the advising and counseling functions, perhaps the weakest link on every major comprehensive research university campus.

The seeds of isolation and the general feeling by the students that they are nothing more than student numbers stemming from inadequate personal attention is a problem that large universities are unprepared to handle, but any willing and resourceful PMS can provide this need. Additionally, the very nature of the military profession enables the military officer to do a better job of teaching than most of his civilian counterparts. Anyone wanting to take issue with this assertion needs only to ask young ROTC graduates who have just attended the Basic Course at Fort Benning, Georgia. They hear flawless presentations delivered by officers who have been schooled in the art of teaching and have rehearsed every spoken phrase before a "Murder Board" of officers skilled in the teaching art. The Military Science Faculty is accustomed to teaching at a level of expertise that would earn the praise of a Cecil B. DeMille, and this alone can enhance the ROTC image and contribute to greater "milidemic harmony" and increased enrollment.

Enrollment is a daily minute-by-minute activity—not something that happens once during the semester. It is a part of the overall mission with which the PMS and his assistant professors must remain obsessed. They can't be everywhere on campus at any one moment, but their enrollment tentacles can extend into every student activity. Every respected organization on the campus is an enrollment asset. Fraternities, sororities, dormitories, honorary societies, religious organizations, bands, athletic teams, student councils, host and hostess type organizations, and the staffs of campus newspapers and yearbooks can be exploited. Nothing is sacred, but the approach must be such that these groups are made to realize that they are the primary beneficiaries. Sophistication and subtlety are key, and it is the leaders or anticipated leaders of these organizations whom the PMS seeks to win over at the outset. Establishing mutual benefit is not too difficult once the goals and needs of these groups are identified. When these relationships are fully established, a student aspiring to be President of the Student Government Association, Homecoming Queen, and the like will realize that achieving such goals are impossible without the support of the corps of cadets. At the University of Alabama, almost every campus leader was enrolled in the Army ROTC program, and most of them ended up being commissioned officers in the United States Army.

Not everyone reading this book will be interested in how to enroll students in ROTC programs on the nation's college campuses, but the most casual of readers may find some of the following guidelines to bear some relation to other activities in which they may be engaged:

» The PMS and his Assistant Professors should eat at the university cafeteria, or at a fraternity or sorority as often as they can swing an invitation. Maximum contact with the student body is a vital part of enrollment growth.

» The PMS, his Assistant Professors, and NCOs must give a friendly greeting to everyone they meet and never pass a group of three or more students without stopping and speaking.

» Memorize the rules for enrollment and retention and

never give an answer the accuracy of which you are not completely certain.

» Go overboard to avoid projecting a hard-nosed, militant, Gestapo image.

» Never tell a cadet or student to come back later. Stop what you're doing, no matter how pressing or important, and provide the necessary help or assistance.

» Embark upon a program to help needy students in gaining part-time employment. If the PMS and his assistants aren't writing hundreds of letters of recommendation, the program is missing out on a powerful enrollment tool.

» Be liberal in administering awards, decorations, letters of appreciation, and publicize them across campus.

» Bestow great authority upon the senior cadets but be sure they know how to use it.

» Never let a cadet or any student on campus hear any member of the ROTC faculty use a dirty four-letter word. If you don't use any such words, no student or cadet will hear them. God's last name is not Damn, and any member of the ROTC faculty who says it is will embark instantly upon a permanent change of station.

» Avoid such words and phrases as "join," "volunteer for," "enlist in," "serve in," "pull a tour in," and "recruit" and "recruiting." Use instead such phrases as "take Military Science," "add Military Science to your schedule," or "enroll in Military Science 101." A phrase such as "join ROTC" carries the inference of a form of commitment. "Take a Military Science course" on the other hand triggers a more favorable reaction. We should not use any language in ROTC that we would not use to describe an English or Algebra class. Students do not "join Algebra" or "volunteer for Chemistry." Hence, they should not be asked to "join, volunteer for, or enlist in Military Science."

These little rules are not only vital for enrolling students in ROTC programs on college campuses, but some of them should govern the conduct of every professor and university administrator in America. Those who lead and teach American youth should set a flawless example for them. Nothing that happens on a college campus is more vital to individual development than is the building of impeccable moral character.

The type of college student that the Army seeks to enroll as candidates for its commissioned officer corps is the type of young men and women who respond in a positive way to demonstrations of impeccable moral character and sense of mission. In retrospect, it was the standards we set, the high goals we pursued, and our refusal to fail that resulted in the success we realized. The University of Alabama spent less money on recruiting in 1974 to 1978 than any of 255 other colleges and universities with ROTC programs, and yet the Alabama Corps of Cadets, became the largest Army ROTC program in America, thanks to a sustained incredible performance of duty by an outstanding group of Assistant Professors, NCOs, and the cadets themselves who became the best "enrollment officers" any PMS could hope to have. What an incredibly-gifted group of young men and women, and it was no surprise to me that scores of them went on to be outstanding career officers in the Army.

Earlier on in 1974 when the Alabama Corps of Cadets numbered only 146, every person associated with the Military Science program embarked on a crusade to become the largest and best ROTC program in America. In those years, the Alabama Crimson Tide, coached by Paul "Bear" Bryant, ruled the college football world. The name of the "Crimson Tide" drew out the best in every player who wore that crimson jersey, and it was a name that no one would disgrace by not giving everything their best shot and then some. I thought that, if such dedication could exist on a football field, then it could be caused to happen in a program where human life and the destiny of the nation were at stake. With no small amount of trepidation, I decided to name the cadet corps "The Crimson Tide of the Army," warning everyone at the outset that the name would be taken away if we failed to achieve the lofty goal that we had set for ourselves. Those special soldiers and cadets saw to it that their PMS would never have to do it.

Adequate numbers of ROTC cadets with the mental, physical, and emotional qualities necessary to become outstanding military leaders were hard to come by in those post-Vietnam years. The enrollment task is not yet as difficult in 2006, but the need for mentally-gifted young men and women of great moral fiber and an abiding love of country has never been so great. The most dangerous world

GOD & COUNTRY FOREVER

in which America has ever found itself demands that the Armed Services be led by the most brilliant, dedicated, morally strong, and courageous young men and women America has to offer. The longevity of the United States rests on the degree to which the ROTC enrollment effort succeeds and on the quality of leadership training they receive.

Successful ROTC programs on the nation's college campuses are vital to the nation's security, and this one fact must never escape higher education or any other segment of American life.

There are Chief Executive Officers of large corporations who receive eight-figure salaries to lead and manage the organization's human and material assets, most of them being greatly overpaid for what they do. While morale, discipline, esprit, and proficiency are accurate indicators of the quality of leadership they exert, "survival of the company" is the bottom line criterion on which successful management is measured. If the company survives, the CEO's longevity is not in jeopardy. By comparison, leadership and management of the human assets of a military organization constitute a fundamentally different challenge. The low pay scales do not permit the use of money as an incentive, and performance depends wholly on the quality of leadership at each level of command. Human life is up for grabs, and the survival of the nation is sometimes at stake. For the military leader, success or lack thereof is measured in terms of victory or defeat. One should gather from the following treatise on "War and the Soldier" that the value of America's fighting men is far greater than the meager pay they receive. Additionally, it should not be lost on America's civilian leadership that the defense of America should not be left exclusively to the poor, the undereducated, the minorities, and the few gifted red-blooded patriots with great leadership ability who voluntarily choose a low station in life, don the uniform, and dedicate their lives to the service of their country. Sadly, the burden lies exclusively with this minute percentage of the American people.

War And The Soldier

March 2001

"I can assure you that a piece of every soldier who died fighting in all of my outfits is grafted on my soul and will remain there from here to eternity."

—Lieutenant General Henry"Hank" Emerson

S OMEONE WHO HAS *BEEN THERE AND DONE THAT* remarked that "When wars happen, the devil increases the size of hell." I believe there is a hell and a devil, and if I'm as right as I think I am, that old architect of evil must surely thrive on the nature of war. He knows that wars have a way of hiding things in the souls of men that remain there imprisoned for all of a man's lifetime—memories of things done for a just and noble cause—but things so nasty, evil, ugly, and distasteful that the psyche holds them forever suspended between a state of purgatory and an inner peace and fulfillment. They remain there, known only to God and the soldier—not so much because they defy explanation—but because the soldier chooses to keep them locked inside his inner being rather than to tell others that within his memories of war are things that hold dominion over his very soul—things to which some soldiers are mysteriously drawn. It is an attraction about which the pundits may theorize but one to which only the great soldiers can relate.

Not all good soldiers are driven to the scene of battle to share the dangers of war with their comrades, but it is the one common thread that runs through the fabric of every great soldier who has held the high honor and unequalled responsibility of leading men in battle. An unwavering love of country, a powerful sense of duty, unreasoned confidence in themselves, and a deep-rooted loyalty to their comrades act collectively and in concert to convince the great soldiers that they belong at the scene of battle so that the job will get done with the least possible loss of human life.

Robert E. Lee wrote that "Duty is the most sublime word in our language; you cannot do more than your duty, and you should never wish to do less." There are those good citizen soldiers, who have answered the call of duty and performed admirably but feel no compulsion to experience it again. Yet, that which they did experience rests at the zenith of the things they treasure most. The American Legion, Veterans of Foreign Wars, and other post-war organizations exist and thrive as much from the memory of war as from patriotism or any other motivation.

One is missing something if they deprive themselves of the privilege of sitting down and talking with a veteran of World War II, Korea, or Vietnam. When they do, they'll learn that there is nothing in the world these old veterans treasure more than the memories of things about war that happened as much as 50 or 60 years ago. I know scores of combat veterans in their 60's, 70's, 80's, and 90's, and you'll learn from being around them that nothing has happened in all of their lives that comes anywhere close to equaling their experiences in the Battle of Midway, the landing on Iwo Jima, the parachute jump into Normandy, the landing on Omaha Beach, the breakout at St. Lo, the one-on-one dogfight with the German fighter pilot, the bloody battle for Heartbreak Ridge, Bastogne, the Pusan Perimeter, Porkchop Hill, the Battle for Outpost Harry, the Kumsong River Salient, Khe Sanh, Tet, or whatever action they experienced. Though many of their comrades died in diverse ways and places, the battles continue in their reverie. For the youngest of them, so powerful is its calling that some devote their lives to the honorable profession of arms, preparing themselves physically, mentally, emotionally, and skillfully to win the first battle of the next war. They wait on the call to fight again, because they see it as their duty and their noble calling, driven by a sense of belonging to a team on whose shoulders often rests the fate of humanity.

There probably never was a soldier who didn't have a passionate hate for one side of war. He has seen what war does to the innocent—the old people, the mothers, and most of all the babies and young children. War takes the lives of the young before their time, and it takes the parents, the homes, the livelihood, and much of the reason for living from those it spares. It is no respecter of age, sex, status, or anything else. The thought prevails that those among the young who fall victim to the bomb and the shell are in a sense more fortunate than many of the others who remain but who have lost everything important to them as a child. The soldier and others would thus be attracted to a "war to end all wars," but such a war is at most a human dream that can be likened unto the Land of Oz that never is and never was.

The facts of history tell us that armies fight better when they have a just and noble reason, but history also tells us that American soldiers will rally behind "Old Glory" regardless of the cause. During the Korean War, the American soldier fought brilliantly despite having only a vague conception of what that war was all about. He fought and died on the mountains and in the mud of that incomprehensible agrarian land while politicians back home divided the country over the very purpose of his fight, telling him that his wounds were all in vain. The majority of the American people agreed with the politicians, but how wrong they were! The backward agrarian half-nation that was South Korea is now a strong, industrial country with a democratic form of government. The South Koreans sent more soldiers to help us in Vietnam than any other nation, and they are one of the closest allies that America has in the world today. What the U.S. soldier did in Korea made a difference in the modern world.

A few years ago, I was persuaded by a Legionnaire to speak on the subject of war at a public gathering in Decatur, Alabama. One of the remarks I made that day was that *I never met a man old enough to have fought in World War II who didn't hate himself way down deep inside for never having served in that war.* It was a war in which every man of military age either served in uniform, had a civilian job deemed vital to the war effort, was rejected for physical or mental reasons, or who was somehow successful in dodging the draft. Those who did serve have had to listen all of their lives to the apologies and excuses that their acquaintances have made over and over just because they never served for one reason or another. After the war, those who didn't serve sought the friendship of the veteran, but in many instances it was not forthcoming. Some felt inferior and others who tried to serve and couldn't felt cheated. They somehow knew there was something they had missed—either their doing of their duty to their country or some ultimate zenith of human experience that they now would never know. They didn't like themselves for it, but it didn't translate into a mad rush to volunteer when the Korean Conflict erupted five years later.

I suppose that there are those who see a degree of insanity in the thoughts and acts of men who are attracted to war, but there are also thoughts of those like John Stuart Mill (1806—1873), the renowned British philosopher and economist, that might be used in their defense. "War, " he said, "is an ugly thing, but not the ugliest of things; the decayed and degraded state of moral and patriotic feeling which thinks that nothing is worth war is much worse." He's right, of course, but even so, the strange attraction that war casts upon some men is a phenomenon that continues to mystify the human mind.

The enduring products of war are personal pride, fellowship, comradeship, and the words of the historians who write about it. That is evidenced by the fact that almost every unit in every war the nation has fought has an association that is kept alive and active by the members of the "old outfit." It explains the hand-wringing and back-slapping when two men from the old outfit meet years later in strange surroundings. A bond of loyalty exists among soldiers of all ranks, from General to Private. It is a bond that survives death, because memories from the fallen linger, and messages continue to flow from their silent bivouacs—inspirational and motivating messages that drive the soldier onward—even into the jaws of death. It is a profound brotherly love that transcends race, background, social status, personality, education, or anything else. These things make a difference to others, but they make absolutely no difference to those who are living in the twilight zone of the battlefield.

A few days ago at this writing, I listened with misty eyes to a cassette tape from General "Hank" Emerson, in my view one of the greatest combat commanders to ever wear the uniform. His men proudly called him "Gunfighter," his radio call sign and a name printed across the front of his command and control helicopter. He told me of a courageous young soldier assigned to one of the companies in the brigade that he commanded as a Colonel in Vietnam. He was a little guy, but when measured in terms of his courage, heart, and fighting skill, he stood as tall as any soldier. Because of his size, he was often used as a tunnel rat, prompting his buddies to call him "Shrimp," and that's what "Gunfighter" called him also. "Gunfighter" frequently dropped by Shrimp's company, commanded by a courageous young officer (Captain Mike Peck) and never failed to have some special thing to say to the fine young soldier called "Shrimp," who already held a Purple Heart and the Silver Star for gallantry. It would be good if I could end the story here as just an example of battlefield comradeship, but unfortunately there's more. In a brilliantly-conducted action that lasted nine days, Gunfighter's brigade literally decimated two main force Viet Cong battalions, killing or capturing almost every man, including the Viet Cong leadership. "Gunfighter" lost only 17 of his men, but even losing such a small number brought no joy to "Hank" Emerson.

The saddest part of the aftermath of battle is the visit to the field hospital where the wounded are separated according to their chances of living. General Emerson never failed to visit the hospital, and upon arriving there after this particular battle in the Plain of Reeds of the Mekong Delta, he was told that he had one man in the "terminal ward." When he walked in, "Gunfighter" was stunned to look upon the bloody face and mangled body of the young soldier called "Shrimp"—arm missing, leg missing, dying—but conscious enough to recognize his brigade commander with whom he had shared the highest respect, a special comradeship, and a common goal. Barely managing to speak, "Shrimp" greeted Colonel Emerson with "Hi, Gunfighter" and moments later said to the best friend he had on earth at that moment, "Sir, I know I'm dying, and I'm scared; Can you stay here with me?" Reaching down and taking hold of the only hand that "Shrimp" had left; "Gunfighter" assured him that he would stay with him as long as he wanted. Moments later, the wonderful little soldier closed his eyes for a minute or so and then opened them long enough to say, "Gunfighter, it's been a honor to serve with you, Sir." When General Emerson had finished telling me that, he said, "My God! Can you imagine that? Hell, it was the other way around!" "A couple of minutes later," General Emerson said, "He was dead, and I had to pry his little black fingers from my hand." At that very moment, if "Hank" Emerson had owned the U.S. Treasury, he would have given it all for the life of that great young American soldier who had given his all for the nation he served. General Emerson didn't say that. I said it for him. What he did say was that "Love is the wrong word to describe some men's attraction to war. No one could love anything that takes the lives of such great young American soldiers that we love and respect so much."

There's an epilogue to this part of the story as well. Captain Mike Peck was wounded severely in the earlier stages of the battle and thought initially to be dead, and General Emerson himself would a few days later suffer severe wounds that would hospitalize him for six months in Walter Reed Army Hospital—wounds that continue to affect him 32 years later. Despite any impressions to the contrary, Generals and Colonels are not spared from the deadly nature of war.

Less than five minutes ago at this writing, I opened a letter from General Emerson in which he was reflecting upon the remarks he had made to me on the cassette tape. *"I can assure you,"* he had written, *"that a piece of every soldier who died fighting in all of my outfits is grafted* on my soul *and will remain there from here to eternity."* That one statement deserves to own a place in the everlasting annals of American history, and I pray that some noted historian will see that it does—if for no other reason than to remind every future private soldier just how much his life is treasured by the great commanders whose lot it falls to lead him into battle.

Had "Shrimp" survived the war, he would be one of those with whom General Emerson would be communicating frequently. Regardless of rank, when a soldier returns from war, he tries to maintain contact with his old comrades. He may have been a General, a Colonel, or a Sergeant, but the truly great ones simply put away their medals and don't flaunt them on their civilian suits. Except for their memories of a time gone with the wind, they melt into society and live as other men. They write letters and sometimes make a phone call, or maybe send a Christmas card. In time they may lose track of an old buddy, but they never

TWO-OLD FADED-AWAY SOLDIERS, LT. GENERAL "RETIRED" HANK EMERSON (LEFT) AND THE AUTHOR MEET AT FORT BENNING, GEORGIA. JULY 2003

forget him, and they never cease to long for the comradeship and fellowship that they knew while playing the ultimate game—a game surmounting the Super Bowl and the World Series—a contest called "war" in which the survival of nations is sometimes at stake and where there are no second prizes for coming in second.

Only a small percentage of Americans have ever experienced war's level of human emotion or lived in an environment wherein the commitment to each other and to the task at hand is total and complete. Had Americans appreciated the soldier as the soldiers appreciated each other and had all Americans been equally committed to victory, the war in Vietnam would have taken a different turn. Americans would not have deserted the soldier and presented Ho Chi Minh and General Giap with a victory that they could not gain militarily.

Most professional soldiers were troubled over Vietnam and its aftermath. It should have taught every potential Captain of the Ship of State and every future Military Service Chief that we should never again send our soldiers to fight any war without a winning objective, where no sanctuaries are granted to the enemy—including neighboring countries. It should also have taught us that we must be equipped and trained to fight every kind of war against any kind of enemy. As essential as these lessons are, however, they pale in the face of another need in America that the Vietnam War laid bare. Americans everywhere need to be taught the true meaning and limitations of *freedom of speech*. It is perhaps America's most cherished right, but it was never intended to include treasonous statements that advocate harm to the nation, its armed forces, or its citizenry. Neither was freedom of speech intended to give demonstrators a right to break the laws of the land or in any way deny other Americans the rights that our Constitution guarantees. Americans must learn that protests and demonstrations should precede the action of the President and/or the Congress to declare war. After the battle is joined, it becomes the duty of every American to stand behind our President and the nation's armed forces until the conflict ends—and to don the uniform themselves if called upon.

More will be said on this subject later in this book. It's so important that double redundancy is not enough.

Another lesson we should have learned in Vietnam is the need to leave the execution of war to those who fight it. In those instances wherein the enemy is void of significant air power, like in Vietnam, speed can compensate for mass and overwhelm an enemy before giving him time to react. Such audacious tactics accompanied by a massive air campaign against the enemy's command and control facilities is a tactic to always be considered. Without adequate command and control, a numerically superior enemy force is rendered ineffective and becomes demoralized. If authority had been given to move swiftly into North Vietnam and take command of the seat of government in Hanoi, the war would have ended successfully as early as 1966. Our failure to do so is a lesson never to be forgotten.

Almost as important as that lesson is one we should have learned but probably didn't. Never again should we send our army into a third world country to fight a war for them while having only an advisory capacity over the host country's forces. *Unity of command* is a principle of war, and either we have authority over their commanders, including the authority to select and relieve, or else we don't become involved.

Such lessons didn't have to be taught to the Service Chiefs on board during the Vietnam era. They well knew these fundamental principles of war, but for whatever reason, they just didn't drive their spears in the ground deep enough and long enough to cause the President and the Congress to give them the resources and the authority to win the war. It was providential that such lessons were not lost on Colin Powell and Norman Schwarzkopf in the months leading up to the Gulf War.

There has never been a great commander who didn't have the guts to speak out, put the good of his country before his own personal advancement, and stand up for the soldiers he commands. Conversely, every soldier lives in hope of serving under a leader that they can respect and trust. In war, they want a General or Admiral who is forever asking what will hurt the enemy the most and then doing it without gambling with the lives of his own men. They expect to be pushed to the limit of their endurance, but they know why—that it's the way to win with the least possible loss of life.

General "Uncle Jack" Deane, who inter alia commanded the 173rd Airborne Brigade in Vietnam is a good example. "Uncle Jack" (his radio call sign) never let the enemy own the day or the night. His battalions were always on the move, seldom ever staying in the same place for more than a day. Under his watch, the 173rd conducted scores of helicopter-borne operations, but he never lost a helicopter on a landing zone—because he placed more value on the lives of his men than he did on the cost of an artillery round or a 500-lb bomb with an instantaneous fuse. He did the things that hurt the enemy most without gambling on the lives of his own men, and his soldiers loved him beyond description.

It is no secret that General George Patton was attracted to war. *He owned the most vital quality a soldier can possess— total self-confidence—utter, complete, and bumptious.* He was audacious and daring, but it was the enemy, and not his men, who were frightened by him. He pushed his men to the limit, but kept saying over and over to his corps and division commanders that "Pushing means fewer casualties; Pushing means fewer casualties; Pushing means fewer casualties! I want you to remember that!" He did the things that hurt the Germans most at a minimal cost in human life.

General Patton knew what it took to win, and one of the things he thought essential might surprise some readers. He believed that victory in war depended on God's blessings. Speaking to his Chief of Chaplains, James H. O'Neill, a few days prior to the Battle of the Bulge in December 1944, he said that "between the plan and the operation, there is always an unknown. That unknown spells defeat or victory. Some people call that getting the breaks. I call it God. God has his part or margin in everything." He had Chaplain O'Neill write him a prayer beseeching God to halt the rains and clear the fog that was making needed air support impossible. A total of 250,000 3x5 cards containing the prayer and a Christmas greeting were distributed to the men of the Third Army with General Patton's order for every soldier to use it and pray fervently. Two days later, with the rain pouring, the German Fifth and Sixth Panzer Armies launched a devastating attack against General H. F. Hodges' First U.S. Army, achieving a breakthrough on a wide front. With the outcome of the war in Europe hanging in the balance, Patton turned his entire Third Army from east to northwest and headed for Bastogne with reckless abandon. On 20 December, to the surprise and consternation of the German Army, the rains ceased and the skies cleared against all weather predictions, and the rest of the story is history. What may not be so well known is General Patton's remarks to Chaplain O'Neill at their first meeting after the battle. "Well, Padre," he said, "our prayers worked. I knew they would." George Patton gave God the credit, and so should we.

General Patton knew that he was drawn to war, and he could never quite explain it, except to say that a great soldier's attraction to the battlefield is embedded in the very soul of man. He once called it the "warrior's soul," which even he could not define and could describe only as a "vitalizing spark, intangible, yet as evident as lightning." Its degree obviously varies from man to man, and there is no way to adequately measure its depth, unless there is a clear possibility that the struggle at hand could end in the death of the opposing participants. *A General is not a prompter on the wings of the stage of war.* Instead, he is *a participant in its mighty drama.* War thus becomes the ultimate test of his moral fiber and the measure of all that God gave him, and I, therefore, believe I am justified in asserting that only those men who have tasted war are ever able to fully comprehend the ultimate *price of victory and the total agony of defeat.*

Soldiers fight to win, and they don't take kindly to seeing their buddies die for no good reason and without the hope of victory. Every battle and every preparatory act leading up to it are conducted with ultimate intensity. Look at their faces when they have taken a hill, withstood a fierce counterattack, sent an enemy battleship to the bottom, or won a one-on-one dogfight, and you will see serene and satisfying expressions that send forth a message that they know that they have been in life's greatest and most important game and won it. Looking at them removes any doubt that Coach Vince Lombardi was right when he said that, "Man's greatest hour, in fact his greatest fulfillment, is that moment when he has worked his heart out for a good cause, and he is exhausted but victorious on the field of battle—whenever, wherever that field of battle may be."

In making a honest-to-God soul-searching self-evaluation of my own personal qualities, I keep returning to the conclusion that man's attraction to war is in some way associated with his desire to do his duty to his country, to measure up, to control and become the master of fear. A strong case can be made that fear is to the courageous men of this world their very best friend, because it enables them to do super-human things. Courage is not the absence of fear but the mental control of it, and when brought under control, it can become the most powerful weapon in the warrior's arsenal.

It is only when men let fear get the better of their manhood that they become cowards. The knees of both the coward and the courageous tremble, but the knees of the courageous will always take them toward the enemy. It was also John Stuart Mill who said that "A man who has nothing for which he is willing to fight, nothing he cares more about than his own personal safety, is a miserable creature who has no chance of being free, unless made so and kept so by the exertions of better men than himself."

It's been said that "soldiers are prepared for war only when they scare the hell out of their own commanders." I think I know what the author of that phrase was trying to say, but I have never seen a military unit that frightened a good commander. Instead, closeness develops between a great commander and his men that is incomprehensible to those who have never experienced it. There is a mutual feeling that between them they own a superior quality and capability—an unbeatable combination. It is this mutual confidence that enables the commander and his men to overcome the natural fear of battle. The result is staying power under stress, cohesiveness, teamwork, and maximum combat effectiveness.

There has always been a great difference between cognition and volition—between knowing what to do and being able to do it. The great commanders know what to do and are able to do it. Yet, the mental and emotional trauma of losing men in battle causes even the greatest of them to eventually begin wondering how many more battles they have left in them. I would imagine that those who are versed in the sciences would say that every man has a breaking point. Even so, the one thing that seems to differentiate among leaders on the battlefield is that the greatest commanders somehow find that they have one more fight left in them.

All of the foregoing having been written by one with no proven unique insight into the human mind, I choose to recognize the reader's right to a different view. The soldier is a product of American society, and except for war itself, it would never have been cast his lot to lay down his life for his country. Summarily, there may be another answer to man's attraction to war, but the recesses of the mind keep sending a message that it is not war per se that attracts the great soldier but instead a deep feeling of noble duty to serve one's God and Country.

The history of war is fraught with the details of great battles dating back to the beginning of recorded history. Military leaders in particular have studied these battles in great detail, hoping that lessons learned from them might in some way aid in winning the first battle of the next war. As a general rule, military units take great care in recording the details of battles and campaigns in which they were engaged. A detailed account, however, of the last significant battle of the Korean War and the emotional impact that the war's end had on the soldiers who fought it do not at this writing appear to have made the history books. It ended in the greatest artillery and mortar exchange in the history of warfare. Knowing of most of its details, I have elected to include a summary of it in this book for history's sake and in remembrance of the great soldiers, living and dead, who experienced it.

A Time and Place That Tried Men's Souls

Artillery rained, white phosphorus fell; seemed surely the mortars were called in from hell!

—SFC Lowe D. Cauble

Company I, 65th Infantry

Author's Note: *Colonel Chester B. De Garve, who would later become a General Officer, is the only person mentioned by name in this account. After 50 years, I would likely miss a few names. So, with sincerest intentions and any apologies that may be due and appropriate, I am attempting, without the use of names, to record a small amount of the 65th Infantry Regiment's actions during the last two weeks of the war. I attempt to write this account, because I've never seen anything except abbreviated references to this action and fear that it might be lost to history, inasmuch as so many who participated in the Battle of the Kumsong River Salient are no longer with us.*

ENDING EVENING NAUTICAL TWILIGHT (EENT) ON 13 July 1953 was not atypical of the onset of darkness during most days of the Korean War. The flashes and sounds of incoming and outgoing mortar and artillery fire and tracer rounds of our Twin 40's were as normal as the coming of night. On all "quiet nights" as 2300 hours approached, the sound of outgoing mortar and artillery fire and the boom of the 90mm tank guns, though deafening in volume, were nonetheless music to the ears, and moments of sleep came to those off-watch or not out on a listening post. However, all in my unit (The 3rd Battalion, 65th Infantry Regiment, Third Infantry Division) knew that the night of 13-14 July 1953 would not be a typical night in that area of the Main Line of Resistance (MLR) near Kumhwa—an area on the western edge of the Iron Triangle (Kumhwa—Pyonggang—Kumsong). No one, though, anticipated just how different that night and the following days would be.

The 65th Infantry had been informed a few days earlier that it would be relieved on line that night by elements of the Second Infantry Division, part of a relief action involving the entire Third Infantry Division. One of the units permanently attached to the Second Division was a battalion from Thailand, and it would be this battalion that would relieve the 3rd Battalion, 65th Infantry. We expected that to be some kind of an experience, because none of us spoke the language. Fortunately, the Thai Battalion Commander spoke English, and the details for the relief had been well coordinated. The relief in place came off surprisingly well, but while it was underway, things were happening big-time in the Kumsong River Valley, located about 15 miles to our east. It was here that the MLR bulged out about three miles, forming a salient in the United Nations (U.N.) line. Amassing seven (7) divisions in the eastern portion of the Iron Triangle, the Chinese had launched a major offensive against a sector of the main U. N. Line occupied by the Capital Division, the elite unit of the South Korean Army. The attack was devastating, and by midnight, the Chinese had overrun the entire Capital Division, breaching their main battle positions. One of the units to be overrun was the United States 555th (Triple Nickel) Artillery that had been assigned to support the Capital Division.

Immediately behind the U.N. line lay a wide valley, running southwest to the Chorwon Valley and then turning more southerly toward Seoul. Mountains lay on each side of these valleys, but there was not an equally suitable defensive position closer than 20 miles to the south of the U.N. line, labeled on everybody's situation map as "Line Missouri." It was this consideration that had a few weeks earlier prompted the orders to company-size units of the Third Infantry Division defending Outpost Harry to "hold at all costs" against repeated Chinese regimental-size attacks.

Needless to say, the seven Chinese divisions massed in the Iron Triangle near Kumsong (80,000 to 100,000 men) and the complete annihilation of the Capital Division in the first five hours of the battle threatened the U.N. units on each flank of the penetration and in fact the tenability of all of Line Missouri. The Chinese advance had to be stopped at the Kumsong River Valley and not permitted to penetrate further into the wide valley leading southwestward toward Seoul. The Third Infantry Division, having been replaced on line that night at Kumhwa was the only division-size force available for commitment against the Chinese onslaught.

At approximately 2300 hours, a call from Colonel Chester B. De Garve, 65th Infantry Regimental Commander, to the Third Battalion Commander (and I assume to his other battalion commanders as well) changed all plans of the 65th Infantry quite abruptly.

Instead of going back into a reserve position for a period of replenishment and training, the 65th Infantry Regiment (about 5,000 men including organic support units) and the Third Division's 64th Tank Battalion (about 800 men) had orders from the Third Infantry Division Commander to move without delay to the Kumsong River Valley, halt the Chinese advance, and restore the east portion of the salient. Concurrent orders went out to the 15th Infantry Regiment to deploy to the Kumsong River Salient, stop the Chinese advance, counterattack, and occupy positions on the 65th Infantry's left flank. Over the years, I have often wondered if that verbal mission statement might have been worded a little differently had the exact size of the Chinese force been known at the time. I have to believe that the commitment of the 15th and 65th Infantry Regiments into the face of the Chinese onslaught had to be made regardless of the consequences, real or imagined, but there would be less confidence in the outcome. Most assuredly, regardless of how much we knew or didn't know of the size of the Chinese forces, the deployment of the two infantry regiments and the Third Division's 64th Tank Battalion to the Kumsong River Salient in the early morning hours of 14 July 1953 was a bold and daring move and one that all expected to be bloody.

The 3rd Battalion needed 38 additional 2 1/2-ton trucks

to transport its Battalion Headquarters, three rifle companies (Item, King, and Love) and Mike Company (Heavy
Weapons) in a single lift. Colonel De Garve was the type
commander who would know that already, and his orders
included authority to commandeer the first 38 trucks traveling the Main Supply Route (MSR), regardless of the unit
they belonged to, what they were carrying, or where they
were going. That was the first and only time in my military
service that I have heard such an order, and one just can't
imagine the difficulty in carrying it out. A soldier having
been ordered by a sergeant or officer in his own unit to
drive his truck somewhere for some purpose doesn't take
too well to being stopped in the dark in a pouring rain and
having himself and his truck commandeered by someone
from another unit. I was one of those doing the comman-
deering, and one can't imagine what such a thing does to
some good private soldier who knows absolutely nothing
about the situation at hand or the legitimacy of the order.

We had commandeered about half of the number of
trucks needed to move the battalion when I received a radio
message to come to battalion headquarters immediately. I
assumed that it was to be a meeting of the company commanders and battalion staff, but the purpose didn't matter.
I was too pleased to be relieved of the task of helping to
commandeer another 15 or 20 trucks. Incidentally, none
of those drivers returned to their own units until after the
war ended. I don't know how their units were informed of
their whereabouts, or if they ever were. There were far more
important things to be done that night and the days to follow, and taking time to notify their units occupied a low

place in the order of things. So, many of these commandeered soldiers, I suspect, were reported by their units as missing in action.

By this time, one of the heaviest rains that I ever saw in Korea was overflowing the ditches and making rivers of small streams. It was far from a perfect night for a relief in place or for the movement of a large number of trucks, tanks, and artillery pieces over the muddy dirt road that led from Kumhwa to the area of the Chinese break-through at the Kumsong River Salient.

There were a few things that no Infantry officer serving in Korea would ever be without. All had a carbine with at least two extra 30-round magazines taped together ("banana-clipped") for rapid reloading, a flak jacket, acetate-covered contour map, grease pencils, flashlight with a pin-head size opening, steel helmet, poncho, canteen, first aid kit, lensatic compass, and a Zippo lighter. I walked in to the Battalion Commander's C.P. armed with all of these and ready for whatever he wanted.

The Battalion Commander did his home state of Georgia proud. He still stands out in my mind as one of the finest combat commanders I've known. He had seen combat in Europe during WWII and was solid as a rock under pressure. I had the highest respect for him and was always careful of what he heard me say. Though more than 50 years have passed, I still remember what he said. His first words were "O'Mary, what do you know about stresses and strains?" I didn't know why he was asking such a question, but I remember answering him by saying, "Sir, probably less than you but maybe more than most." He chuckled at the answer and then asked me "Does that mean you know how to read a map in the dark?" I don't remember how I responded, but whatever I said prompted him to tell me that he was sending me along with the S-1 (Personnel Officer) to a spot he pointed to on his map to reconnoiter an attack position that the 3rd Battalion would occupy as a place from which to launch a counterattack against the Chinese penetration. The location was several hundred yards south of the spot where the U.S. Triple Nickel Artillery had been overrun a few hours earlier. He told me and the S-1 to "Get up there, pick out a good attack position, meet us on the road and lead us in. Don't waste any time. We've got to get there before the 'Chinks' do."

Quickly, I measured the road distance and wrote it in grease pencil on my acetate-covered map, and as soon as I had recorded the jeep's odometer reading, we were off to the Kumsong River Salient. In combat, jeeps don't have tarps (except for trailers), and windshields are laid forward on top of the hood. Vehicles use only cat eyes that are of no help to a driver in seeing the road. The cat eyes are safety features that can be seen by others during the hours of darkness, and therefore accidents are often prevented. Watching the odometer, wiping water off my map and looking at it with a pin-point flashlight, observing valleys and mountain peaks from the light given off by exploding artillery and mortar rounds, and confirming our location along the way by other features such as streams and forks in the road, we made it to the attack position in less than an hour. On the way, we met unidentified soldiers afoot (never knowing at first sight if they were Chinese or South Korean Army and a few vehicles heading south) but neither going nor returning did we see anyone moving northward. Neither the 15th Infantry nor the 64th Tank Battallion had at that hour departed Kumhwa. It goes without saying that the muddy road from Kumhwa to the Kumsong River Salient was not a very comfortable place to be on that dark, rainy night of 13-14 July 1953. There were a couple of knee-knocking incidents on the way back from the Kumsong Valley that required a little luck, but the S-1 and I made it back to Kumhwa moments before the battalion was ready to depart. Having made it there and back, I felt good on that morning of 14 July 1953.

Beginning Morning Nautical Twilight (BMNT) would come and go with the 3rd Battalion, 65th Infantry on the move. The heavy rain that had fallen all night long suddenly ceased and the light of day made things easier. Despite the fact that I had not slept in more than two days and nights, I thought it was a good day to be a soldier.

A wide valley runs from Pyonggang (not to be confused with Pyongyang, the North Korean capital) southeast to the Kumsong River Valley. It was from this same area that the Chinese launched a major offensive in April 1951 that resulted in a general U.N. withdrawal to positions around Seoul. Whether a déjà vu was the objective this time around or whether the Chinese wanted to convince South Korean President Sigmund Rhee that he should agree to a truce is a question that only the Chinese can answer. The real objective might have been a combination of the two, considering the massive force that the Chinese had assembled.

Having annihilated South Korea's Capital Division,

the Chinese had advanced to positions located along the base of the Kumsong River Salient. It was here that the Chinese were met with the first of several tank forays by the 64th Tank Battalion that provided valuable time and protection for the remainder of the division, led by the 3rd Battalion, 65th Infantry, to occupy battle positions south and southwest of the Kumsong River Valley on reasonably good defensible terrain. Encountering the first of the forays, some of the Chinese lead elements stopped and started digging in, apparently in preparation for fresh troops of one or more of the remaining divisions to pass through their positions and continue the advance.

By this time, the 15th Infantry had occupied positions on the 65th Infantry's left flank. W.F. Strowbridge, a 3rd Division historian, would later record that *"Fighting reached an intensity not seen on the Korean battleground since 1951."* He further stated that the Chinese were stopped cold when they ran up against the Third Infantry Division—in which the 15th and 65th Infantry Regiments held their ground and *"inflicted tremendous casualties on the enemy."* The foxholes and trenches hastily dug by the Chinese forward elements became their grave.

With the arrival of better weather, U.S. Sabre Jets and B-29 bombers were in the air from first light to near darkness inflicting untold damage to the thousands of Chinese troops, vehicles, and supporting weapons caught in the open area of the Iron Triangle. In the meantime, the 3rd Battalion of the 65th Infantry advanced northward from its attack position, tied in with the left flank unit of the South Korea's Second Division, and solidified a large portion of the forward edge of the salient. By the afternoon of 17 July, the threat to the entire MLR had been reduced—but not eliminated. In the meantime, our Sabre Jets, B-29 heavy bombers, mortars, and artillery kept hammering away at the exposed Chinese troops.

Then, on the morning of 18 July, the 64th Tank Battalion was ordered to conduct a spoiling attack against the enemy positions in the southwest portion of the salient. Company A penetrated the enemy's forward positions and continued their advance until attacked by Chinese infantry. Using their own individual weapons, the tank crews fought off the attacking infantry and subsequently continued their advance, uncovering a Chinese assembly area, and inflicting heavy casualties upon the enemy. The spoiling attack proved to be a huge success, complementing the 65th Infantry's actions to consolidate its defensive positions in the east half of the salient. The massive Chinese force had been stopped cold by the 15th and 65th Infantry Regiments, the Third Division's 64th Tank Battalion, an incredible amount of artillery support, and unrelenting air strikes against the huge massed, exposed, and unprotected enemy force concentrated in the wide valley passing through the Iron Triangle. The Chinese had lost about 28,000 men. Despite the price, the Chinese could claim a limited victory. Their attack had destroyed the elite division of the South Korean Army and overrun the United States 555th (Triple Nickel) Artillery.

From 18 to 26 July, the 15th and 65th Infantry Regiments worked feverishly to improve their defensive positions. The sounds of interdictory mortar and artillery fire continued unabated around the clock, and good weather enabled U.S. air strikes to continue at an uninterrupted pace. The Chinese were paying an ever-increasing price for their actions, but they weren't finished—not just yet.

The last day of the war was one that no American soldier at Kumsong will ever forget. Word came over the Armed Forces Radio Network a little after 1000 hours (10:00 A.M.) on the morning of 27 July (and a little later through command channels) that a formal truce had been signed with the Chinese at Panmunjom. A ceasefire would commence at 2200 (10:00 P.M.) that evening, and both sides would withdraw a certain distance (either two or three miles as best I remember) from their present positions and create a de-militarized zone across the entire Korean Peninsula from the Sea of Japan on the east to the Yellow Sea on the west. All weapons, ammunition, and other materials and instruments of war would be removed.

I'm doubting that the task of carrying away the ammunition that the Chinese had stockpiled had anything to do with their decision to use the truce as an opportunity to initiate a mortar and artillery battle unequalled in military history. I know it was not a consideration in our case, because we had the transportation to move it. Moreover, our artillery positions lay outside the area to be evacuated.

The Chinese may have thought they had more ammunition than we did, since they had conducted a deliberate build-up and that we had moved without warning. For whatever might have motivated it, the Chinese decided about noon to "airmail" everything they could package up and send out way. The official estimate was that the 65th

Infantry received over 20,000 rounds of artillery from the Chinese guns in addition to twice that many 82mm and 120mm mortar rounds—all arriving on the afternoon of 27 July. We returned the courtesy by airmailing that many and more in their direction. Not wanting to be outdone, South Korea's 2nd Division on the 65th Infantry's right flank joined in the action. Needless to say, the Chinese were receiving an abundance of airmail on the afternoon of 27 July. The greatest artillery and mortar battle in all of history had occurred after a ceasefire had been agreed upon by both sides.

By the time the sun started to set, some of the ground occupied by the 65th Infantry looked like an impact area. There had been a lot of digging deeper while the exchange was taking place. Otherwise, far more casualties would likely have occurred. One can draw some satisfaction from the fact that 28,000 Chinese were killed and twice that number wounded, but in no way does that reduce the pain of losing a single American soldier. The official total U.S. casualty count of the units participating in the Battle of the Kumsong River Salient was 297 killed, 910 wounded, and 88 captured by the enemy. In retrospect, I think that I can say without contradiction that the most audacious of soldiers would ever want to experience such an incredible firepower exchange after winning or losing was no longer an issue. As a very minimum, the ears of the participants will never again permit them to appreciate a Beethoven symphony.

When an eerie silence fell upon the battlefield at about 2145 hours on the evening of 27 July 1953, there was no celebration, no smiling, and no shout of victory. Yet, if one had seen the expressions on these same soldiers' faces when they had earlier taken a hill or withstood a fierce counterattack, they would have seen expressions that sent forth a message that they had been in life's greatest and most important game and won it.

When daylight broke the following morning, Chinese soldiers in large numbers had emerged from their hastily-dug foxholes. Thousands of them had died, but it was evident that those who remained outnumbered the men of the 65th Infantry. It was a weird experience to see enemies staring at each other with no weapons aimed and no sounds normal to war.

It took awhile for all of us to realize that the war had not ended in a tie—that South Korea still existed, a vital interest of the United States had been protected, and that 35,000-plus American soldiers had not died in vain. The last few weeks of the three-year conflict, beginning with the bloody battle for Outpost Harry and ending with the mortar and artillery exchange in the Iron Triangle at Kumsong, had been a time that tried the soul of the American soldier. He measured up in every way at every moment, adding his page to the storied history of the America patriot, and in the end he had to think that the result was worth the price he paid.

HOW WOULD YOU ANSWER THESE QUESTIONS?

» What does "Duty-Honor-Country" mean?

» Does being a citizen of the United States of America require our undivided loyalty to her?

» Does being an American obligate us to serve faithfully in the nation's Armed Forces if called upon?

» Should there be a mandatory penalty for giving aid and comfort to an enemy of the United States in wartime?

» Can words alone constitute treason?

» Except when directed by competent authority, should travel to an enemy homeland in time of war constitute an act of treason?

» Should every proven act of treason require punishment under Federal law?

When you have finished reading this book, return to this page and answer the questions again. Some of you may well respond differently. The following article dealing with American Democracy could alone change one's viewpoint.

A Democracy Test
That America Flunked

It is rather for us to be here dedicated to the great task remaining before us.

-Abraham Lincoln, 19 November 1863

A S STATED IN THE PREFACE TO THIS BOOK, SUR-vival of a democratic system of government rests upon the unwavering support of a nation's citizenry. The degree of its enduring strength depends upon a thorough knowledge of its working parts and a commitment by the people to protect the way of life that a democracy makes possible. Where either is lacking, a democracy crumbles.

The year was 1973, and the American people had just completed a long, comprehensive examination on Democracy—a test that began almost 12 years earlier and ended when the last helicopter cleared the airspace over South Vietnam. It had been a practical examination, a hands-on experience, that Americans had been expected to pass easily. Instead, they failed miserably—with most never having realized that a test of the fabric of America had taken place.

Even after 33 years, the grades have not been officially posted, because those primarily responsible for the substance of recorded history—the media, the politicians, and the professors—have been involved in a concerted effort to redefine and alter the standards, tenets, and meaning of American democracy so as to make the questions fit the response, thereby giving themselves a passing grade. In the process, the very foundation of American character has been questioned, shaken, and uprooted. The time-honored principles that had governed the conduct of Americans since 1775 were suddenly unpopular and obsolete. Honoring the principles meant flunking the test. So, good became bad; patriotic Americans became enemies of hearth and home; and the participants in the "immoral war" in Vietnam were cast as unintelligent beings, murderers, and social outcasts. So great were the degrees of dismay, confusion, and mental and emotional stress experienced by the Vietnam veterans over the hostility shown them by their own countrymen that thousands were unable to cope with the mental and emotional cataclysm that engulfed them. As the symptoms of the so-called "Post-Vietnam Syndrome"—suicide, divorce, alcoholism, mental and emotional instability—began to surface, the same Americans who caused the phenomena to happen in the first place set out to exonerate themselves by asserting that the cause emanated from a "guilt complex" stemming from the soldier's experience in Vietnam. This widely-claimed and unchallenged cause of the Post-Vietnam Syndrome served only to pour fuel on a raging inferno already out of control.

Every soldier who has seen the whites of the enemy's

eyes in more than one war knows clearly that there has never been a moral war and that the same physical, mental, and emotional stresses existing in one are present in all. The color of the mud and the color of the blood remain the same, but that fact could not be known to most young men who fought in Vietnam. Most were not even born until after World War II, and they were babies in their mother's arms when the truce was signed at Panmunjom to end the Korean Conflict. They had grown up during an era of prodigal plenty as part of a permissive society in which the family unit had been torn asunder. The feeling prevails that they were consequently less prepared mentally and emotionally to withstand the unmerciful treatment they received at the hands of their own countrymen. They fought brilliantly and courageously as soldiers in an environment where they were viewed and treated by their commanders with respect and humility, but many could not later endure in an environment that treated them with hatred, scorn, and rejection.

The cause of the so-called Post-Vietnam Syndrome is incontestably clear. It was caused by Americans in America—not by experiences in Vietnam. The mass emotionalism and anti-military sentiment triggered by the media, ultra-liberal college professors, Hollywood activists, and left-wing politicians, beginning principally with the Tet Offensive of 1968, had a profound mental and emotional impact on the young Americans that had answered the nation's call. They were the most loyal and patriotic of America's youth, but they were deserted by their own countrymen. Many couldn't handle the unconscionable treatment they received, and a host of mental and emotional problems engulfed them like an avalanche. Many of them became so confused that they began to believe that they had somehow committed a crime by serving in Vietnam.

The assertion that the problems experienced by the Vietnam veteran resulted from a guilt feeling for answering the nation's call and fighting in Vietnam ranks at the top of the most cruel acts ever to be perpetrated on the American soldier. Those who make that charge or believe in its validity continue to blow the same examination that they have been flunking since 1968.

The behavioral scientists tell us that all behavior, good or bad, stems from some effort on the part of man to satisfy a human need. If this is true, then it logically follows that the actions of nations emanate from a perceived need to either protect a national interest or further a national aim. There must, then, be a cause for every venture—be it a mutual security pact, trade agreement, cultural exchange, or an act of war. In the case of Vietnam, the involvement of the United States was not without just cause. It is not, however, the intent here to underwrite the assertion that preventing a North Vietnam takeover was a vital interest of the United States, but it would be irresponsible silence if one failed to state that the Vietnam War was more justified than some other wars that this nation has fought, World War I and the Mexican War being prime examples.

The die was cast in Vietnam when Ho Chi Minh refused to abide by the spirit and intent of the 1954 Geneva Accords and permit campaigning by all candidates throughout all of Vietnam in a fair and free election. Instead, he insisted on an election wherein he would be the candidate for North

Vietnam, where the population was almost double that of South Vietnam and where 99 percent of the voting population would be led to the ballot box. No candidate from South Vietnam could have possibly been elected. South Vietnam would be turned over to the Communist Camp in North Vietnam without a struggle, and neither President Eisenhower nor our friends in South Vietnam could hardly be blamed for not agreeing to such conditions—although one can purchase several books, authored by anti-war American professors, that relate only half-truths, while blaming President Eisenhower for the fact that the elections never took place. These architects of knowledge flunked a course in intellectual honesty for reasons they should have to explain to the American people.

Ho Chi Minh would have agreed readily to the elections—if they could have been conducted under his terms. In reality, however, he never held out much hope that President Eisenhower, Diem, et. al. would be so naïve. This explains why he left his Viet Cong infrastructure in South Vietnam at the time his main force units were moved northward in a deceptive compliance with the Geneva Accords. The Viet Cong infrastructure, having already been schooled and trained in guerilla warfare and insurgency operations, needed only to receive their marching orders.

Though unschooled in counterinsurgency operations, the United States came to the aid of a helpless friend—initially by providing military supplies, then advisors, and subsequently combat troops in escalating proportions. Whether the American effort to prevent a military takeover of South Vietnam was just or unjust may be academic in some circles, but what is not so academic are our self-imposed limitations on the use of force, granting of sanctuaries for the Viet Cong and North Vietnamese Army, and failure to see the war through to a successful conclusion. Though no direct role was played by most Americans in these tragic decisions, the influence of millions had a decided impact on them. The violent adverse reaction to the American excursion into an area of Cambodia occupied by only the Viet Cong and North Vietnamese Army is testimonial to the impact of public opinion on the conduct of the war. The army was pulled out of Cambodia before it could make a dent in the enemy's sanctuaries.

The American living room was given a daily dose of war scenes from South Vietnam with language that suited the purposes of the networks. The media, the ultra-liberal professors, and the politicians quoted each other, in the process ridiculing or completely ignoring any scenario or voice of opinion that tended to support the cause of the conflict, applaud the military effort, or express faith in ultimate victory. Americans responded as might be expected. Just as they had responded positively to the propaganda campaign to prepare the nation for World War II, Americans would respond negatively to the propaganda campaign to turn them against the war in Vietnam. In each instance, the outcome of the war was in direct proportion to the degree of media and political support.

Fundamentally, it is the right of the American people to choose for or against any war, but once a choice has been made to commit American soldiers in battle; our system of government cannot endure a change of mind or course in the midst of the conflict. Except when suddenly attacked or when the nation is immediately endangered, commitment of American soldiers to battle should follow a declaration of war by the Congress of the United States which formally commits the American people to support the war from onset to ending. Likewise, if an American president is forced by a situation to act without a formal declaration by Congress, the American people are equally committed to support the war. In either instance, once war is cast upon us, it becomes folly to talk peace until the war is concluded successfully. That Americans turned their backs on the young soldiers that the duly-elected civilian authority sent away to war is a dark chapter in the history of the republic, and it must never be permitted to happen again.

The behavioral scientists are probably correct in theorizing that there is a cause behind all human actions, but a case can also be made that American behavior goes deeper than a conscious motive. Americans have an inherent superiority complex and a penchant for quick decisions. Patience, tenacity of purpose, and a willingness to undergo long-suffering are foreign to the national psyche and character. Herein rests the nation's Achilles Heel, and it is perhaps the single greatest reason why Americans flunked the Democracy test in the late 1960's and early 70's. Had the war ended in 1966, as it most surely would have if the military had been given full rein, there would have been no anti-war demonstrations, no rebellion against an "immoral war," no massive disobedience to government, no treasonous flights to Canada to avoid service to country, no anti-military sentiment, and no drab memorial in Washington that the anti-war element point to as "a sobering reminder of how right we were." More importantly, far fewer American soldiers would have died, and those who did would not have died in vain. It is the contention here that our political leadership flunked the test, because they neither understood our own American mind, the mentality of the North Vietnamese, nor that wars of insurgency can last indefinitely under conditions that grant the enemy a sanctuary. When the war did not end promptly and decisively, it was too much for the American ego, and what followed is a well-known scenario.

By the time of the Tet Offensive of 1968, the media had begun to write its own history of the war, refusing to print the battlefield reports coming out of Vietnam without attaching negative connotations upon them. The Tet Offensive was made to look like an American defeat, when in fact it was one of the most lop-sided military victories in all of history. Militarily, the North Vietnamese Army and the Viet Cong had suffered a tremendous setback that would have proved disastrous had they not gained so many allies inside the American homeland. The American Press, scores of professors and politicians, and thousands of spoiled college students seizing upon the opportunity to avoid service to country presented Ho Chi Minh with a political victory that he had not been able to gain militarily. The American psyche and penchant for quick decisions had taken on an active face—frustration, impatience, disobedience to government, and hatred of and rebellion against our own military forces.

ROTC buildings on college campuses were burned to

the ground. Viet Cong flags were paraded down Constitution Avenue in the nation's capital city. Demonstrations by faculty and student groups disrupted the educational processes on college campuses across the land. Federal highways, streets, and thoroughfares were often blocked by lawless groups. Thousands of young Americans fled the country to avoid being drafted into the Army, and many more deserted the armed services. Political leaders and others fanned the flames of emotion and dissent for political or personal benefit. There were university professors, who had authored books on Democracy and International Relations, and politicians a break or two away from becoming President of the United States actively involved in pressuring the military forces to quit the war in Vietnam—to rebel against the duly-elected civilian authority.

The nation had withdrawn its support for the soldiers it had sent to war. The American homefront hated them for doing what American soldiers had been praised for doing in all of the nation's previous wars. President Lyndon Johnson, who had won a landslide victory in 1964, lost the confidence of the American people and would not run again. President Nixon would pull our forces out of Vietnam; leaving the South Vietnamese to defend themselves in a war they had no hope of winning against the Soviet-backed North Vietnamese regime. The South Vietnamese reaction to the North Vietnamese offensive that immediately followed, launched by thousands of soldiers who were only 11 and 12 years old at the time of the Tet Offensive of 1968 was exactly what the American military had predicted.

If there is ever an intellectually-honest history written

of the Vietnam War, it is not likely to be kind to either Lyndon Johnson or Richard Nixon. Lyndon Johnson made most of the mistakes, and Richard Nixon elected to preside over the first American defeat in the 199-year history of the republic—a political defeat, not a military defeat, but a defeat nonetheless. There is cause in many minds to forgive Nixon for abandoning the South Vietnamese. The argument goes that the situation he inherited from Lyndon Johnson left him no alternative but to try a honorable way out by "Vietnamization" of the war. The bottom line, however, was that he did have the alternative of lifting the restrictions that Lyndon Johnson had imposed and permitting an American invasion of North Vietnam as well as the entry of American forces into the portion of Cambodia east of the Mekong, and into eastern Laos along the Ho Chi Minh Trail. With associated naval action to close the port of Haiphong and the Mekong River and fighter and bomber support to prevent aerial re-supply, the war could have been brought to a successful end in as little as 90 days. Nixon, however, chose the popular option: Get out!

The decision of the United States to lose the war was something new in the American story. The choice was unilateral and voluntary, and it was new to history that a nation winning militarily could lose a war through its internal mistakes and moral decay of its people. Peace came without honor, and this should, and does, disturb the very soul of every patriotic American.

If the good people of America are frightened that this great nation is capable of doing what it did to the people of South Vietnam and Cambodia, they ought to be more frightened over the total disregard that Americans showed for their own system of government. In the massive effort of millions of Americans to cause the military to succumb to the emotionalism that gripped the majority of the American people and pull out of Vietnam against the will and directions of the President of the United States, we see a troubling story that tried the souls of most military career professionals.

Unwittingly and unknowingly, these Americans were attempting to get the military to participate in the destruction of our republican form of government. It is providential for the nation that its professional military men knew and understood the consequences of the actions of their fellow countrymen. They chose to continue to fight a war they knew would be lost politically at a future time. Instead of fighting to win a war made un-winnable by the limitations imposed, our soldiers in Vietnam were now fighting a war to preserve the American democracy—and it was an easy choice for these professional military men to make on behalf of their fellow countrymen. Their efforts were met with hatred and scorn, but they held fast to their Oath of Allegiance to "preserve, protect, and defend the Constitution of the United States against all enemies, foreign and domestic." Had they forgotten that oath and elected to quit the war in Vietnam, they would at that moment have taken the final step in fulfilling the prophecy of the haters of freedom who have long contended that one day our republican democracy will crumble.

The millions of Americans who sought to destroy the military's will to execute the war and rebel against civilian authority were in fact asking the military to assume more authority than an army can have in a democracy or even in a Communist dictatorship. Armies that can rise up and topple the government through an arrogant display of military power or simply refuse to remain subservient to civilian authority constitute a military dictatorship—something that is repugnant, unacceptable, and foreign to American thought. Yet, this is precisely what many of the nation's political figures, thousands of university professors, and millions of others from all walks of life were attempting to do. The nation's professional military men did not let them succeed, and ironically it was the hated military arm of government who held the democracy together at a time of its greatest trial in the history of the republic. In so doing, they enjoyed their finest hour at the time of their lowest public image.

Those who dispute the idea that such a misdirected effort was made should objectively analyze why there was no Post-World War I Syndrome or Post-World War II Syndrome—wars of far greater immorality in which millions of innocent people died. More importantly, they should reflect on what the nation might be like had they been joined in their actions by the Armed Services. Once they do this with true intellectual honesty, they just might begin thanking God for the men and women who never let them succeed.

Americans under age 65 cannot possibly envision what the American home-front was like in World War II or what makes those in our late 70s, 80s, and 90s feel the way we do. The Baby Boomers and Baby Busters have never known an America that was totally united behind a common cause. In fairness to them, the survival of the United States has not been at stake in any war fought during their lifetime. The intent of a Veterans Day 2002 speech the author delivered at Gordo, Alabama was to honor the nation's veterans, but it was also designed to educate the young on what it takes to build a stronger, safer, and better America. I include it in this book in the most fervent hope that America will never again flunk a course in American Democracy.

Veteran's Day Speech at Gordo, Alabama

Greater love hath no man than this: that he lay down his life for his friends. .

John 15:13, *The Holy Bible* (KJV)

I PUT AWAY THIS OLD UNIFORM WHEN I RETIRED ABOUT 25 years ago, but I've been persuaded to wear it today. It's still in pretty good shape, and my cap and shoes still fit. If you should ask me what these ribbons and medals are, I might miss a few of the exact titles—but there's one among them that all of you old soldiers recognize. It's the World War II Victory Medal. It was awarded to every soldier who served in uniform prior to the end of hostilities. I didn't do a whole lot to earn it, but I walked among a lot of great soldiers who did. They were my heroes—all of them. I was privileged to serve under some of those great soldiers after the war, and even after 57 years, I still remember most of their names.

I remember the American home-front, too. Mothers worked in defense plants or were at some place in the community rolling bandages without pay. Almost no one had any money, but they had endured the Great Depression and knew what it meant to survive on the bare necessities of life. The destiny of America was a stake, but that generation of Americans were tough. They knew the price that had to be paid, and they were prepared to pay it. Thousands of young men didn't wait to be drafted. They volunteered for no other reason than to help save their country. It certainly wasn't the pay. The salary of a private was $21 a month. Many of them even lied about their ages, and their parents let them do it. A lot of young men died at age 15, 16, 17. Those kids and their moms and dads earned the right to be called "The Greatest Generation." Tom Brokaw was right on track in his assessment, except that he was describing two generations rolled into one.

A couple of months ago, I attended a reunion in Arlington, Virginia, with a group of old veterans who served a few years after the big war in the Third Infantry, more commonly known as The Old Guard or President's Honor Guard. Many of that old bunch have gone on to the Great Bivouac in the Sky—some dying of old age and some having come home in a body bag from Vietnam. Except for me, all of them had grown old since I last saw them. That old bunch had been responsible for interring their comrades in Arlington Cemetery, guarding the Tomb of the Unknown Soldier, guarding the White House, performing ceremonies and conducting protocol activities for foreign dignitaries, and a whole host of other things. We owned a deep-rooted pride in what we were doing and total loyalty to each other, and what happened at that reunion let us all know that the closeness we knew back then had only grown greater over the years. There was a lot of hand-wringing, backslapping, and some wet cheeks.

We took a bus tour of that special old place. On the way to visit the Tomb of Unknowns and some gravesites of our old buddies in Arlington Cemetery, we passed by the Marine Memorial. It is a perfect example of why I have trouble sorting out the differences in Veteran's Day and Memorial Day. As you know, the Memorial shows six young Marines planting Old Glory on the summit of Mount Suribachi on Iwo Jima in March of 1945. Most Americans, I think, see it only as six nameless Marines raising a flag on the top of some hill they had captured. It's more than that—far more than that.

The young Marine putting the pole in the ground is Harlon Block. He was an all-state football player, and all of the seniors on his high school football team enlisted in the Marine Corps a day or two after graduating. He died on Iwo Jima after planting that flag, holding his intestines in his hands. He was 19 years old.

The soldier next to him is Rene Gagnon. If you had been there and had taken his helmet off the day that flag was raised, you would have found a photograph of his girl-friend. Gagnon put it there for good luck. He was 18 years old, and maybe in some way that photograph gave him the extra courage he needed to fight and survive. He walked off of Iwo Jima, but 5,000 young men from the 3rd, 4th, and 5th Marine Divisions didn't.

The next Marine is Sergeant Mike Strank. He was 24 years old, so old in fact that his men called him "old man." From those who knew first-hand, he never talked much about death and killing to them, because he knew his men were just little boys. Instead, he always said things like "You do what I say, and I'll get you home to your mamas." The "old man" didn't make it home himself. An exploding Japanese shell "tore a hole in his chest and ripped out his heart." He died the most merciful way—instantaneously.

The next soldier is Ira Hayes. He was a Pima Indian from Arizona. He also walked off of Iwo Jima, and President Harry Truman said to him sometime later in the White House that "You're a hero." A few minutes later, Hayes said to a group of reporters, "How can I feel like a hero when 250 of my buddies hit the island with me and only 27 of us walked off alive?" He suffered mentally and emotionally from the loss of his buddies and from a feeling that he had no right to survive. Years later, he died dead drunk lying face down at the old age of 32.

The next young man is Frank Sousley from Hilltop, Kentucky. He died on Iwo Jima at the age of 19. A barefoot boy carried the dreaded telegram to the Sousleys' house, and their next door neighbors, who lived a quarter of a mile away, could hear Frank's mother screaming throughout the night.

The next young man you see in that memorial is *John Bradley* of Antigo, Wisconsin. One of his sons, John Bradley, Jr., tells us in his *Flag of Our Fathers* that he lived until 1994 but never gave an interview in all of the 49 years he lived after the war. He trained his sons to tell telephone callers and others who came to his house to interview him that he was away on a hunting or fishing trip. His job on Iwo Jima was that of a medic. He held many young boys as

VETERAN'S DAY SPEECH AT GORDO, ALABAMA

they died, but he never saw himself as a hero. He told his sons, "There's one thing I want you to always remember. The heroes of Iwo Jima are the ones who didn't come back."

So, three of those six young men on that Marine

FIRST FLAG COMES DOWN. | SECOND FLAG GOES UP, PLANTED BY MARINES HARLON BLOCK, JOHN BRADLEY, RENE GAGNON, IRA HAYES, FRANK SOUSLEY, AND MIKE STRANK. | THE FIRST FLAG TO FLY ON MOUNT SURIBACHI, PLANTED BY MARINES JOHN BRADLEY, HANK HANSEN, CHUCK LINDBERG, JIM MICHAELS, BOOTS THOMAS, AND PHIL WARD.

Memorial walked off of Iwo Jima, three died there, and the haunting memories of the loss of his buddies killed one of them later just as dead as if a bullet with his name on it had come his way on Iwo Jima. Knowing who those six young soldiers were and what happened to them makes the memorial come alive when you see it, but it will also cause you problems as to what to say on Veteran's Day if you are called upon to say it. I find it impossible to limit our honors this morning to just the ones who walked away. I either read or heard a statement someone made about all those white crosses one sees in a military cemetery—that they were symbolic of a crucifixion of a sort—that *someone whose remains lie under that cross, someone very young usually, has died for someone else's sins.* It's usually the sins of a tyrant like an Adolph Hitler or a Saddam Hussein whose lust for power wouldn't let him leave other countries alone. But sometimes it's also the sins of national leaders with good intentions. Don't for one brief moment believe a history book that tells you that 4-million people died in WWI, because some student shot an archduke in Sarajevo—or believe any book that says we got involved in the war over some phony issue like freedom of the seas. William Jennings Bryan resigned as Secretary of State in 1915, because he kept telling Woodrow Wilson that his public utterances were going to get us in war. They did.

Well, we're here today to honor the veterans, and we're going to do that, because they deserve to be honored—all of them who served honorably from the Revolutionary War to the present day. America was born at the point of a gun—the soldier's gun. Our real birthday is not July 4, 1776, but instead it's October 19, 1781. That's the day that George Washington's begrimed and battered soldiers took the measure of Cornwallis at Yorktown, Virginia, and gave birth to the United States of America. If Cornwallis had kicked our tails at Yorktown, the Declaration of Independence might be just another piece of paper trampled under the feet of the tyrant in the sands of time. It wasn't signed on the 4th of July anyway. Most signed it in August, and the representative from Delaware didn't sign it until 1781. Please hear this! I'm not denigrating the importance of the Declaration of Independence. It needed to be written and was a landmark in human history, but all of us need to remember that our independence was won by blood, sweat, and tears—not by words inscribed on a piece of parchment, regardless of its quality.

It was the soldier who gave birth to America, and it has

been the soldier who has kept this nation free for the 10-score years that have come and gone since that 19 October 1781. Sometimes, it was just a patriot's dream set afire by an ideal. Sometimes, it was the love of Old Glory, each other, the esprit of mutual confidence and devotion. Sometimes, it was just the doing of a job that had to be done regardless of the cost. There have been times when the measure of the soldier was less his bravery in battle than his ability to simply endure. He endured—but not for glory or reward. What the people of America must remember is that this nation was *born in arms, purged in blood, and made secure by sacrifice.* We could have a holiday like this one every month of the year, and we wouldn't even then be able to thank the veteran enough. And while we're doing it, *we need to thank those red-blooded Americans who didn't serve in uniform but never wavered in their support of the soldier, regardless of how they felt about some war that the soldier had been sent to fight.*

It pains me this morning to have to say that the majority of the people of this great nation have not followed the example set for them by the American home-front in World War II. Had Americans behaved in World War II as they behaved during the Korean Conflict, the Vietnam War, and the way we're behaving right now, the boundary line between Nazi Germany and the Imperial Japanese Empire would be a north-south line drawn through the geographical center of the present-day United States.

Reflecting upon it, I'm reminded of a four-line poem that someone wrote sometime somewhere:

God and the soldier all adore

In time of war but then no more;
When wars are over and all is righted,
God is forgotten and the soldier slighted.

That's what began to happen a few years after WWII with one exception: Neither the soldier in Korea nor Vietnam ever enjoyed the adoration of the people of America. Korea and Vietnam were wars *that demanded everything from a few and nothing from so many.* I walked among those soldiers, and I know they deserved more at the hands of their countrymen. Given the attitude of the people back home, I am astonished at what those soldiers did and puzzled at why they did it.

I'm astonished, because they were fighting and dying without knowing why. When I taught Leadership at Fort Benning, Georgia in the mid-1950s, I often quoted from Eric Severeid's tribute to the Korean War veteran. I wish now that I had kept a copy of his exact words, because he had a way of saying things that no other news commentator in my time has been able to equal. I remember his saying that the greatest mystery about the war was what made America's young soldiers fight so long and so hard for a cause they couldn't even identify. He pointed out that there have been armies over the centuries who fought well only for glory and victory, but such did not apply to the Korean Conflict. Neither did it apply to the Vietnam War. There have been armies, he said, who fought well only when their homeland was invaded, but that didn't apply to our soldiers in Korea. We can now say the same for our soldiers in Vietnam. There have been soldiers, he said, who fought well out of some burning moral or religious zeal, but our soldiers in

Korea had only the dimmest conception of what the war was all about. Such was even more so for our soldiers in Vietnam. In both Korea and Vietnam, our young *soldiers fought and died in the mud of those bleak and incomprehensible lands while politicians at home divided their country over the very purpose of their fight, telling them that their wounds were all in vain. They fought ahead, knowing that while allied nations were cheering them onward, they could see their so-called allies coming to help them in no great numbers.* They fought ahead under rules that would not let them win, living the worst life they had ever known while their countrymen back home were living the best life they had ever known. *They knew it was too much trouble for their countrymen back home to walk to the nearest blood donation center. So, they gave their own blood to their wounded comrades.*

There are some words in *We Were Soldiers Once and Young,* by Lieutenant General Hal Moore and War Correspondent Joe Galloway, that put a frog in my throat and a tear in my eye. Referring to our young soldiers in Vietnam, they wrote, with great emotion I'm sure, that those wonderful young men "killed for each other, died each other, and wept for each other . . . their world often shrank to the man on their right and the man on their left and the enemy all around. For those who lived, the country that had sent them off to war was not there to welcome them home. The America of World War II no longer existed . . . our people had come to hate the war . . . and those who hated it the most—the politically sensitive—were not in the end sensitive enough to differentiate between the war and the soldiers who had been sent to fight it . . . They hated the soldier as well, and there was nothing left for those magnificent young Americans to do except to hit the ground in the crossfire just as they had learned to do in the jungle."

I wish I could answer the question this morning as to how each of these young men were raised up and why they behaved so magnificently. They certainly weren't feeding on the examples set for them by the overwhelming majority of their countrymen. I can only surmise, as Eric Sevareid did, that the answer lies deep in the heart and tissues of American life, but none among us can unravel all its threads. The answer, he said, must surely have something to do with their parents, their teachers, their churches, their scout troops, and their neighborhood centers, but I think it also has to do with the quality of those who led them and their explicit unreasoned belief in themselves as soldiers, committed to give all they had for what they had come to believe was the greatest nation to ever exist upon the earth. Whatever was responsible, it goes without saying that their behavior transcends the performance of those soldiers of history who fought out wars of certainty and victory. What they did *was something new in the American story and something that must be viewed with respect and humility.* Make no mistake about it, no red-blooded American could have walked among those young soldiers without loving them beyond description.

Just in case there is any misgiving among anyone here this morning as to how officers in our armed forces look upon the ones they lead, let me say this: I've been an officer; I've been a sergeant; and I've been a private soldier, and I can tell you that there is a profound brotherly love that exists among soldiers of all ranks from General and Admiral down to the lowest-ranking private or seaman. It is a love that transcends race, background, social status, personality, education, or anything else. These things make a difference to others, but they make absolutely no difference to those who are living in the twilight zone of the battlefield.

As Joe Galloway wrote, "*Hollywood always gets it wrong.*" But they finally got it right when they filmed *We Were Soldiers*. If you haven't seen that movie, go buy a videotape of it. There's not an ounce of untruth or embellishment in it. Mel Gibson plays the part of Lieutenant Colonel (later Lieutenant General) Harold G. "Hal" Moore, Commander of the 1st Battalion, 7th Cavalry—and he does it superbly. You students of history will remember that the 7th Cavalry was the unit commanded by former Major General (then having been demoted to Lieutenant Colonel) George Armstrong Custer in the ill-fated Battle of the Little Big Horn. No such defeat happened to the 7th Cavalry this time. In the first major battle by U. S. Forces in the Vietnam War, you will watch a story unfold that depicts how the deep-rooted love and loyalty that soldiers of all ranks have for each other brought a great victory over the North Vietnamese Army.

Well, there's a lot to say about the veteran and never seemingly enough time to say it. Permit me, though, to say these things in closing:

There can be a great difference in love of country and patriotism. All but a few Americans love this country, but the overwhelming majority love it, because they love its milk and honey. Yet, they aren't willing to give anything of themselves in return for the milk and honey it offers. The words were written a long time ago that "Freedom isn't free." Those are true words, but it is only a few who pay the price. Freedom is free for 95 percent of our people. When we eliminated the draft, we pre-ordained who would die in war—the poor, the undereducated, the minorities, and the less than one-half of one-percent who love this country so much that they voluntarily devote their lives to serving America in uniform. As I speak to you this morning, I can tell you that almost none of the bayonet-in-the-gut Infantrymen undergoing basic training at Fort Benning, Georgia, come from families in the top third of the income scale. If you go down there to find sons of the rich and the white collar educated, you had better take along your lunch, because you'll get awful hungry before you find one. *The absence of a draft is an awful moral wrong that should haunt the souls of us all.* Yet, no candidate from either political party can say so and be elected President of the United States.

The bottom line to what I'm saying is my deep belief that a lesson of history needs to be etched indelibly upon the very soul of every American. *Great nations and great civilizations have fallen, because the people of those nations lost the will to fight, the desire for self-sacrifice, or the necessary dedication to their country and the way of life it represented.* The very ultimate in the ideals of patriotism, respect for tradition, duty, honor, the desire for self-sacrifice, and faith in Almighty God must be found in the hearts and minds of all Americans. They are the only things that will keep this nation free. Yes, I mention God, and I make no excuses for it. God led us through World War II. We trusted in Him.

Every soldier carried a Code of Conduct card, and it bore the soldier's signature. It instructed the soldier that if captured he was to give the enemy only his name, rank, serial number, and date of birth. The last line on it carried these words: "*I will trust in God and in the United States of America.*" Such a message to a soldier is not possible in 2002, but whether something is legal or illegal will never change my deep conviction that *any court of law, judge, or political party that in the name of justice and equality is willing to remove God from the fabric of America is more to be feared than an army of millions or any number of international terrorists.*

I ask each of you to seek out our soldiers and the veterans who still live and thank them for doing what only they can do and have done. *The American soldier is your faithful servant and bodyguard. Our service men and women defend you and your family, and sometimes they die doing it. You owe the soldier and the veteran for everything you enjoy in America, and you have as much responsibility to serve this country in uniform as they do.* Think about it and then go and seek them out and thank them while they're still with us. The time for many is growing short. They're dying at about 1,300 per day, and I thank each of you gathered here this morning for permitting me to speak in their behalf.

Many families of veterans were gathered that day at Gordo, Alabama. In fact, it has been a lot of years since I have seen a whole community of patriots completely united behind our Armed Forces. There were several hundred people there that day, and they all seemed to know each other. They were just one big family, and the thought occurred to me that they had something that most communities don't have. The family unit that had always been the citadel of America's strength had somehow survived in Gordo, Alabama. What I saw that day prompts me to include the following item in this book.

THE FAMILY: CITADEL OF AMERICAN STRENGTH

Son, remember who you are and never do anything to reproach the family name.

—William Thomas O'Mary, 1945

ETTER MEN THAN I HAVE SOUGHT TO UNCOVER the road to greatness and failed, and there have been others who were great men and women and didn't know it. They simply lived life as they thought best, doing the things that seemed consistent with what they had been taught by their parents and what they understood to be right in the eyes of their God. These men and women put their families before themselves, and they placed no limits on the degree of sacrifice, including death, that they were willing to undergo for their family, their country, and their God. My father was such a man. He was a self-made mining engineer, builder, and a great mathematician. I never thanked him enough while he lived, but I was able to acquire some land on which he was born and gave it to the University of Alabama to name an endowed scholarship in his memory. The Will T. O'Mary Memorial Endowed Math Scholarship is the first endowed math scholarship ever to be established at the University of Alabama. Because of the way endowed scholarships are managed, his name will be called frequently for as long as the University of Alabama stands as an institution. Buildings will crumble and landscapes will change, but endowed scholarships will live in perpetuity. That is a chilling thought and a great way to honor my father's memory, but it doesn't compensate for the things I didn't do and say while he lived.

I have kept the words in one letter I wrote to my dad from Vietnam. It may have been the only one. An Infantry officer in combat has little time to write to anyone, including his wife and kids, but somehow you're able to fit one in among those you sometimes write to the next-of-kin at a moment when you're the loneliest man in the world. It was several years after the Vietnam War that I received a letter from Congressman Tom Bevill of Alabama expressing his condolences over my father's death and enclosing a letter I had written on 7 September 1967 from somewhere in Vietnam. He had somehow acquired a copy of the letter and had read it into the Congressional Record. When I read my own words, I learned again that men can cry. I had thanked my dad when he may have needed it the most. I hadn't remembered writing it, but there are few things that I've done in my life that I'm equally glad of doing.

I share some of that letter with the reader for several reasons. One reason is my deep conviction that we must never forget the role our fathers played in forming the nation they passed to us—a nation of high morality whose people truly believed that the longevity of the United States of America rested upon the sovereign hand of God. A second reason may be little more than a guilt feeling stemming from the fact that I haven't told others enough about the giant of a man I had for a father. A third reason is to leave no stone unturned that will help build a stronger, safer, and better America by building a new character into the people of America through strengthening of the family unit and restoring the eroded moral fiber of our land. No other path will take us there, and the end of America's longevity is certain unless we succeed. The following are excerpts from my letter to my father and its presentation to Congress:

(Mr. Bevill: Mr. Speaker, Lieutenant Colonel Paul R. O'Mary of Nauvoo, Alabama, in the Seventh Congressional District, is serving in Vietnam. He is the son of Mr. and Mrs. Will T. O'Mary. On his father's 70th Birthday, Lieutenant Colonel O'Mary wrote home. His letter is very timely—and very refreshing. It focuses upon some simple truths that are, I believe, most important.

Mr. Speaker, I insert Lieutenant Colonel O'Mary's letter in the Congressional Record and commend its contents to the close attention of my colleagues:)

Nauvoo Man's Birthday Present:
A Letter Home from Vietnam

"Dear Dad and Family: Well, Dad, it's your birthday, and I hope it finds you well and healthy. It isn't every man who can work as hard as you have and still be able to do the things you do at the young age of 70. As I look back on the 40 years that I've shared with you, I can say that not one of those years has been easy. Every dollar that found its way into the house was over-earned in terms of sweat and toil. Yet, as hard as every penny was to come by, everyone

of us knew you would give all you had simply for the asking, and whether we really needed it or not made no difference.

There are other things I remember—like how you never fenced us in, but rather trusted us to do what was right when you weren't around—how you taught us right from wrong—to have to lay it on us occasionally, but for the most part, we did what was right—usually out of respect for the dearest dad on earth—and a mother who loved us like no other mother could, and one which causes all of us to give thanks to the origin of our birth. What I am now or will be in the future, I credit to you and Mom.

THIS PICTURE OF A CAR-BIDE LAMP, COTTON SCALE, AND STEEL TRAP ARE SYMBOLIC OF DAD'S LIFE. HE WORKED IN THE COAL MINE THE YEAR AROUND, FARMED IN SEASON, AND TRAPPED FOR MINK AND MUSKRAT DURING THE WINTER THAT REQUIRED GETTING UP AT 4:00 A.M., NEVER HAD A VACATION IN HIS LIFE AND DIED OF BLACK LUNG AT AGE 82.

I remember when I was quite young, I used to look up at the stars and wonder what those heavens had seen, what they would see, and what they would bring to me. Many moons have passed since then, but sometimes the present situation in which I find myself causes me to still look up in the sky and ask the same questions—and dream the same dreams. Doing this never fails to deepen my appreciation for my upbringing and bring a clearer understanding of my reason for being on this earth. I ask myself where I am and where I'm going. I go over the day's events and tomorrow's mission—its nature so trying that I sometimes wonder if I'm up to it. But my thoughts always drift homeward to my first family—and to my wife and kids. It is only then that I see clearly where I am, where I'm going, and what my purpose in life must be. It is then and at times like these that I remember my heritage—a heritage that was built by men who had no concern for themselves personally—but chose instead to sacrifice themselves so that their children and children to be born might have a better life. I remember how you did that for us, never sleeping beyond 4:00 in morning and often working at two or three things just so we could eat. Just thinking about it makes what I'll face tomorrow a lot easier.

Dad, you had your dreams, too, and you can always be sure that, when you look back, you know that you gave your all to make them happen. And, Dad, they did happen. We may have to fight wars, but we don't have to work and slave the way you did, often without adequate food or clothes.

Dad, you've done your job on this earth. I just hope your sons can do half as well. Unfortunately, we did not inherit all of your abilities. The most that we can possibly achieve is to find contentment, but we can, as you taught us, respect the achievements of everyone else. Dad, you taught us that when our journey ends a man has been a man if he can look back and say that he did his best. I'm not sure if I can ever say that, but, Dad, I believe you can.

So, Dad, today my thoughts are with you, and this letter has a deeper purpose than to just wish you a happy birthday. It is to send you my love and my everlasting thanks for being my Dad."

That, I think, was the first and only time I ever told

Dad that I loved him, and I don't remember his ever using the word to describe his feelings for me. Yet, I don't think that anyone ever loved his wife and children more than "Buddy Bill," a name that the men in our little town most often called him. What we did often hear him say was to "Never fail to stand up for the family, protect each other, and never do anything to disgrace the family name." "If you give everything your best shot," he would say, "that's all that a dad can ask." I remember his telling me once to "Be careful of the ones you pick for your close friends. God tells us to be careful of the company we keep. Only bad can come from running with bad company. Son, never start a fight, but if one is forced upon you, let the one who does it know that he picked on the wrong boy. If you have to, fight him every time you see him until you beat him. Once you've put a good whipping on him, he'll never pick another fight with you or anyone else, and no one else around here will ever again pick on you either." The time would come to follow Dad's guidance on two separate instances, and I learned the wisdom of his words.

Over a period of time beginning with World War II, the family unit has all but disappeared from the fabric of America. Fathers are in a state of confusion, and millions of young men across America grew up in fatherless homes. As the 21st century unfolds, over 40 percent of our children are living in homes without a father. That figure is up from 17 percent that existed as recently as 1960, and the percentage grows daily. A good case could be made that the most urgent domestic problem facing America in Year 2007 is the absence of responsible fatherhood. Even in those homes where fathers reside, there is rarely a lofty vision of manhood that is compelling to the man of the house. America is in trouble, because the family unit is broken and needs fixing. The Holy Bible is the one source of instruction that tells us how to fix it, but only a small percentage of America's fathers turn a serious ear to the tutorship of the Scriptures.

God instructs us in His Holy Word to obey His commandments and to raise our children according to the example set by Christ Jesus. Not one time in all of human history has our Lord deserted His children, and He instructs us in His Holy Word to never desert our own. In our marriage vows, we promise God that we will remain united *"until death do us part,"* but only a small percentage of the last two generations of Americans seem to know the meaning of a promise, pledge, oath, or vow. Vows seem made to be broken, and marriage is obviously viewed by many as the cause of divorce. Knowing that half of all marriages fail, thousands avoid the legalities by simply cohabitating out of wedlock. *"When the new wears off of their crystal chandeliers,"* many of these go their own way as well, but these temporary unions and permanent separations aren't reflected in the statistics. The impact, however, remains the same—deserted children, deadbeat dads, problems for society, and further erosion of the moral fiber of the American people.

Individualism and selfishness have gained dominion over the American psyche and replaced the sense of responsibility to God and Country that existed two generations ago. Much of this troubling condition finds its roots in the deterioration of the oneness that characterized the American family.

Civilization has not seen a world so dangerous as the one that exists in 2007, and never has the need been greater to rekindle the deep-rooted love and loyalty to God and Country that was so firmly anchored in the family unit. The need of a national crusade to restore the eroded moral fiber of our land has never been more urgent, and it must begin now before the erosion grows deeper.

We may not want to admit or accept its reality, but there is a war underway on our planet that neither diplomacy, foreign policy, nor even a self-imposed isolationist strategy can bring to an end. It is a war that the United States will win or lose—a war with no realistic hope of an armistice or ceasefire. It will end in victory or defeat, and the result will be total, final, and irrevocable. It promises to be the longest war in human history—a type of struggle that does not bode well for any nation or people with a penchant for quick decisions. The United States owns such a penchant, and it remains our Achilles Heel. That's the bad news. The good news is that the only way that America can lose is to fail to stay the course regardless of how long the struggle lasts.

Our enemies are convinced that American resolve will eventually begin to wane just as it did during the Vietnam War. As troubling as it is to say it, at this writing we are already hearing enough anti-war rhetoric to strengthen the enemy's confidence in the eventual outcome. Summarily, Americans have an urgent problem on our hands. We have some fixing to do, and the problem has to do with our hearts and minds. We can't relocate our families near their old country homes as they once were and work on family unity, but we can begin to teach patriotism, sense of duty to society, responsible citizenship, morality, Americanism, and commitment to the Judeo-Christian principles that until now have made and kept our nation free. I'm not a high school principal, but if I were, no student would don a gown and mortar board in my high school until he or she stood before me personally and recited the American's Creed with a look in their eyes and an expression on their face that left no doubt as to whether he or she meant it.

Parents and teachers of young children have an awesome responsibility in deciding what young children ought to be taught. There are, of course, times when the choice may not exist. Textbooks and teaching materials selected by the state govern the teaching content, but much teaching is optional. For example, though most don't realize it, the teachers who require their students to memorize "Invictus," as I was required to do, are teaching atheism. Likewise, every teacher must know that teaching Darwin's Theory of Evolution is teaching atheism and undercutting the Judeo-Christian principles that are embedded in the moral fiber of America. I ask you to study carefully the following abbreviated article on "What Parents and Teachers Ought to Know." It won't make you an authority on Darwin Mythology, but it will equip you to oppose it at every opportunity.

WHAT PARENTS AND TEACHERS OUGHT TO KNOW

"See to it that no one takes you captive through hollow and deceptive philosophy . . ."

—Colossians 2:8, *The Holy Bible* (NIV)

THERE ARE SOME THINGS THAT WE SIMPLY HAVE to know if we are to avoid being victimized by deception and false teaching. *The Holy Bible* (Ephesians 6:11, 14) calls this "putting on the full armor of God . . . with the belt of truth buckled around your waist." Unfortunately, this wise counsel from the Apostle Paul has never been read by some and has gone unheeded by too many others. Hence, the world has been victimized in the 20th Century by false teaching rendered in the deceptive name of scientific knowledge. God's armor has been cast aside.

Though most Americans believe that God exists, we have stood by idly and watched the atheists take command of the reins of government and institutions of learning. Atheism governs an American society that has undergone a profound moral decline in a single generation. It logically follows that we should ask ourselves what caused millions of

Americans to self-destruct morally and spiritually. I believe that question has one primary answer that pales any other by comparison. The root cause is the widespread acceptance and teaching of Charles Darwin's Theory of Evolution as "fact" in the public schools of America.

My own high contempt and disdain for Darwin's Theory of Evolution compels me to refer to it as "Darwin Mythology," and that's the name I give to it orally and in writing. The mythology begins by asking us to accept the assertion that life itself came not from God but from the chance occurrence of chemicals in some body of water eons ago. This is as far back as the Darwin Mythologists can go, because they find themselves unable to explain how the hydrogen and oxygen atoms that formed the water may have originated from nothing—from a complete void. Starting with a single living cell, all forms of life, Darwin says, began to develop through *chance mutations* and *natural selection* across millenniums and eons of time. It's all an incredible fairy tale, but when such is taught as "fact" in the public schools of America, God and the Bible become irrelevant to millions of school children, who keep being told over and over by atheistic liberals that *"It's your body, and you have a right to do with it whatever your mind says do."* Therein rests the onset of the moral and spiritual bankruptcy that has come to pass.

When I was an Infantry officer in the Army, I became obsessed with the need to prepare myself to win the first battle of the next war. So, I quit reading about the Civil War and went to school on the tactics, weaponry, and relative combat power of the Soviet Army, considered to represent the greatest threat to the United States at that time. Likewise, when it became abundantly clear that the teaching of the Theory of Evolution as fact was destroying the moral fiber of America, I reasoned that I had to learn about a different kind of "enemy" of the United States. I studied Darwin's *Origin of the Species"* and read from the textbooks being used to teach our youth. The more I learned the more certain I became that *natural selection* has never happened since the beginning of time and that no species ever evolved into another. No fossil ever uncovered substantiates that a transition from one species to another has ever happened—not even once. Yet, the Darwin Mythologists are obviously able to dupe each other and their helpless students with the simple explanation that the absence of a fossil in no way indicates that the transitory species didn't exist. They just didn't leave evidence of their existence, the Darwinist dupers contend.

We are seeing the publication of some books that expose the fallacy and impossibility of Darwin Mythology. One such book in particular deserves to be read in our public schools, but don't count on its getting there. The book is titled *Tornado in a Junkyard: The Relentless Myth of Darwinism.* Its author is James Perloff, a former atheist turned Christian. He states in the book that *when the so-called "fact" of evolution was sold to him by his teachers, God and the Bible had no chance with him.* Perloff is a baby boomer and relates in his book why his generation bought Darwin Mythology so easily. When the teachers started telling them that the Bible was a fabricated hoax, they *concluded that the myth included the Ten Commandments and God Himself.* Kids could then set their own standards of behavior, and that's exactly what they did. The Darwin Mythologists had found it increasingly easier to persuade thousands of their gullible students who had already become morally degenerative.

I remember spending part of a day in 1981 with a distinguished professor from a very reputable northeastern university, a two-time Pulitzer Prize winner and alumnus of the University of Alabama. He had earlier written in an essay how he had been introduced to *Evolution* by Dr. Ralph Chermock, a graduate of Cornell University who came to the heart of the Bible Belt in 1946 with a new Ph.D. in Entomology (science about insects)—well-armed with *"the latest theories of evolution."* Chermock is described in the essay as having *"proceeded to inspire students"* with his teaching, many of whom went on to be professors like himself. How teaching *"theories"* could be inspirational is difficult to grasp, but apparently Chermock's enthusiasm for the subject and the way it was presented led many students to accept Evolution as scientific fact. Sadly, their gullibility made them easy victims of the *deadly disease of moral decay* that Evolution spreads rapidly, and unlike the nation's reaction to Typhoid Mary, there has yet to be a quarantine imposed. Thousands of the baby boomer generation contracted the disease and passed it through their children to their grandchildren. It takes longer for Evolution to kill than Edgar Alan Poe's "red death," but it's even more deadly because it attacks the soul of man and brings on spiritual death.

The latest statistics reveal that increasing numbers of teenagers entering college as believers in God are either avowed atheists or agnostics by the time they graduate. That Jesus said *"I give unto them eternal life . . . and no man shall pluck them out of my hand"* (John 10:28, KJV, The Holy Bible) gives reason to conclude that those young students falling victim to Darwin Mythology neither had a personal relationship with Christ Jesus nor were they ever in His hands. Even so, the Darwinist professors of our time are striking some mighty blows on behalf of the master they serve (the devil to most, "Old Scratch" to my mom). Few, if any, of the young men and women they have persuaded to believe in *"Evolution"* will ever come to know Christ Jesus as their Lord and Savior.

It should not be lost on the Darwin Mythologists and their student victims that believing in Evolution is following in the footsteps of three of the most evil and notorious men in the history of the world. Karl Marx, co-author of *The Communist Manifesto* and author of *Das Kapital,* two of history's most evil and cruel manuals on how to gain power and enslave the human race, used Darwin's *Origin of the Species* to push his Godless Communist doctrine. Josef Stalin welcomed Darwin's Theory of Evolution, taking comfort from the thought that with no God there would be no eternal consequence for murdering millions of his own people and banning the Bible from the Soviet Union. Adolph Hitler was such a staunch disciple of Darwin that he sought to evolve a master race in his notorious Third Reich.

In America, our university professors have fallen victim to their own egos, embracing the most morally-damaging theory to be formulated in recorded history and espousing it as fact to the impressionable helpless students under their tutorship. Most of the Darwinists are supreme egotists, and to ever admit to being as greatly mistaken as they are would be too damaging to their professional reputation. Their egos are so great that some have resorted to intellectual dishonesty in an effort to give credibility to the Darwin myth and enhance their own professional reputations. That teaching Evolution can only lead to an immoral world doesn't seem to curtail their atheistic effort.

In truth, the Darwin Mythologists have the cart before the horse. They admit that nothing can emanate from a vacuum. They have no explanation as to how nothing became something, how the first component of the first cell emanated from a total void. Neither can any Christian explain how God created everything, or how He has always existed, but simple faith relieves them of the burden. How so many so-called intellectually-honest scholars can embrace a theory of creation by chance without explaining the origin of the raw materials from which the creation occurred remains one of the most mind-boggling mysteries of our time. How they can convince others of its validity is an even greater mystery.

In the "search for truth," published theory most often takes precedence over published fact. Darwin's *Origin of the Species* is a good example of how far-fetched some theory or subject may be and still gain credibility in the academic world. It transcends the human mind that no established fact, truth, rule of law, proven principle, or exact science has equaled the impact that Darwin Mythology has had on modern civilization. Judeo-Christian America has stood by and permitted an indefensible theory to replace the mere mention of God in the public schools across the land.

If the ideals of Americanism are to be embedded in the hearts and minds of the young, they must be told the truth in all things. There's nothing wrong with teaching theory as long as it is identified as such. It is a crime of monumental proportions, however, to expect students to distinguish fact from fiction. Young students are helpless, vulnerable, and powerless to discern the truth or control what they are taught when they have no background in the subject. Except in the rarest of cases, they are without authority and in no intellectual position to judge the validity or reliability of what they read in their textbooks and experience in the classroom. The only safeguard against being victimized by such false teaching is the preparation that parents can provide. *If every young person in America is prepared to challenge their teachers to explain how the first living cell evolved from a total vacuum, their parents have taught them well.*

The author's strong conviction and expressed conclusion that the Theory of Evolution is fallacious and morally wrong should in no way be interpreted as asserting or inferring that all Darwinist professors are practicing intellectual dishonesty and know that they are teaching a false doctrine. Obviously, some believe what they are teaching, despite the fact that a true application of the Scientific Method will forever fail to prove its validity. Darwinists should, therefore, admit to their students in both the printed and spoken word that Darwin's Theory of Evolution falls short of proven scientific fact. Such a statement would in no way shortchange the teaching objective or process. Our young people would still learn as much about Darwin Mythology as they presently do. Then sometime somewhere the Darwinists might come to realize that belief in God is the one thing that can enable them to teach Darwin Mythology without destroying the moral fiber of America.

If the Darwinists continue to call Evolution a science and teach it as a scientific fact, Christendom is left with only one good alternative: *Fight for the enactment of a Federal law requiring Evolution to be taught as an elective only, being neither commingled with any other discipline, nor required for graduation—such law to apply to both secondary and higher education.* Evolution could still be taught, but our young people would no longer be forced to hear it.

Talking to people about God has one limitation that all must appreciate and observe. We cannot go so far as to pressure anyone to listen. Just as freedom of speech has its limitations, talking about God likewise has it boundaries. At the outset, permission must be granted by the person(s) to whom one's remarks are directed, and at no time can statements be made that are degrading, embarrassing, or threatening. Speech is one of our most treasured freedoms, but it is also the most misunderstood, as the following exposition relates.

FREEDOM OF SPEECH

Freedom-of-speech is a treasured right of every American, but it does not extend to treasonous statements or spoken words that either endanger or advocate harm to the people of the United States.

THERE IS GROWING EVIDENCE ACROSS OUR BELOVED land that the true meaning of "Freedom of Speech" is misunderstood by almost all of us. One hears oft-repeated statements from patriotic Americans to the effect that "I don't agree with your protesting against the war, our President, and our fighting men and women, but I will defend to death your right to do it." Such statements assume that freedom to protest in any number of ways has no limitations as to time, place, and circumstances. That, Mr. and Mrs. America, is a monumental error and a complete disregard for the inherent responsibilities of every citizen of the United States. It is tantamount to saying that citizenship carries no responsibility to country.

The American's Creed is not a law, but it is a statement of the principles to which responsible and loyal Americans at one time subscribed. The House of Representatives approved it in 1918, and prior to World War II it was part of what 7th and 8th grade students were taught in Civics class. Although more than 60 years have passed, I have never forgotten the words in that creed. To me, it was not just a creed but a solemn commitment to one's family and to the United States of America and all it embodies. This is what it says:

> *I believe in the United States of America as a government of the people, by the people, and for the people—whose just powers are derived from the consent of the governed—a democracy in a republic, a sovereign nation of many sovereign states, a perfect union, one and inseparable, established upon the principles of freedom, equality, justice, and humanity—for which American patriots have sacrificed their lives and fortunes. I therefore believe it is my duty to my country to love it, to support its Constitution, to obey its laws, to respect its flag, and to defend it against all enemies.*

These words clearly tell us that we are to obey the laws of our land, that we are not to engage in acts of civil disobedience, that we are all equal and that we will not engage in activities that infringe on the rights of others, like blocking a public road or highway to prevent others from passing, that we will not burn or disgrace the flag of the United States, that we will love America for the right reasons—not just for its milk and honey—that we will not side with a foreign power, and that we will serve our nation honorably in uniform if called upon to do so.

It is not possible to live by *The American's Creed* and do or say things that serve the purposes of an enemy of the United States. Once the President and/or the Congress have made a decision to wage war against a foreign enemy, all protesting and demonstrating against the nation's leadership and our military forces must come to an abrupt end. Once the battle is joined, there must be *"a perfect union—one and inseparable."* It is a folly of the first magnitude to protest and demonstrate against a war once the battle is joined. Such is the surest way to lose the war. The time to protest and demonstrate ends instantaneously with the decision to fight, and never at any time should protests be directed toward the men and women sent to fight the nation's wars. That is like going over to a county courthouse to protest some local tax law and do so by beating the living daylights out of the janitor. Americans must learn to differentiate between wars and those sent to fight them. An indisputable case can be made that protests, demonstrations, and such treasonous acts as fleeing to Canada to avoid the draft can and do result in the death of American soldiers at the hands of an enemy whose will to fight and persevere are boosted by such activities. Jane Fonda, for example, was just as effective in killing American soldiers in Vietnam as was any Viet Cong or North Vietnamese soldier armed with an AK-47. Actions and rhetoric that boost an enemy's faith in ultimate victory and cause him to persevere are as deadly as a well-aimed weapon with great killing power.

Even before the onset of war, there are limitations on "freedom of speech." As the old saying goes, freedom of speech doesn't allow us to "yell FIRE in a crowded theater." If one did so and people were injured or trampled to death in a wild exodus from the theater, the yeller would likely be arrested and charged with a felony. By contrast, during the war with Iraq, Professor Nicholas de Genova stated in a speech to 3,000 people at Columbia University that "the real heroes in America are those who will do everything they can to help defeat the military forces of the United States." He also stated that he would "like to see a million Mogadishus." In other words, he wants to see 18 million American soldiers die, and he's not the only one. There are dozens of professors in our institutions of higher learning peddling the same poison. If you're willing to take a chance on becoming so frightened that you can't sleep at night, go purchase a copy of David Horowitz's book, *The Professors*. You won't find any acceptable freedom of speech in what some of these "professors" are saying to their students and to anyone else who will listen. You'll find instead that what they're teaching covers a spectrum that ranges from immoral to evil to criminal to high treason, and it boggles the mind that they are walking the streets and continuing to be paid in American money to encourage impressionable college students to hate America and work toward our downfall.

Then, there are the two women in California who carried a banner during an anti-Iraqi War demonstration, stating that "WE SUPPORT THE SOLDIERS WHO FRAG THEIR OFFICERS." There is no way under Heaven to justify such horrible words as being freedom of speech. These two women and university professors like Nicholas de Genova and Ward Churchill are dangerous domestic enemies of the United States. If I were recruiting terrorists or espionage agents to do their dirty work in the United States for some foreign power, I wouldn't have to look very far, would I? But why should anyone pay for undercover espionage when it is being done overtly at no cost to America's enemies?

There are those who seek to justify their rhetoric and activities in time of war by saying that "*I support our soldiers. I just don't support the President or the war. The war is wrong, and our soldiers shouldn't be there.*" Many take such a stand, including large numbers of our elected members of Congress, apparently failing to understand that one can't support our soldiers without supporting their Commander-in-Chief, who just happens to be the President of the United States. Once again, such people need to be reminded that anti-President, anti-war rhetoric and all other activities of a similar ilk must end the moment the nation goes to war. Politics ends when war begins. Fortunately for the nation, only a small Fifth Column failed to support President Roosevelt in World War II. Otherwise, freedom of speech wouldn't exist in this land, and neither would the United States of America.

There are those who expect to be able to do, refuse to do, or say anything, regardless of how damaging it might be to the United States, and they are "appalled" at being called "un-American" for doing it. "Un-American," however, is an appropriate adjective. It describes any American who can neither embrace nor live by *The American's Creed*. It includes all who would refuse to don the uniform of the American soldier if and when the nation calls, their opinion of some war notwithstanding. *The American's Creed* is the yardstick by which responsible citizenship and patriotism are measured, and those who would take issue with its validity are exhibit #1 to the type of person who deserves the description of "*un-American.*"

Given the greatness of the United States of America, the ideals and principles for which it stands, and the way of life it makes possible for its people, there would appear to be no identifiable motivation for anti-Americanism on the part of anyone in our beloved land. We hold that the people of some nations hate America, because they aren't free and don't like us because we are. That seems to be true, but it doesn't explain why there are those from within who seek to do harm to America. The only logical explanation is that in some misguided way these people believe there is nothing worth their personal sacrifice. They are shallow creatures who would ordinarily have no chance of living in freedom unless it is made possible by the sacrifices of others. The overwhelming majority of them never served a day in the Armed Forces, and they will find a way to never do so. They are only willing to protest and demonstrate, and they want to lump everything they do and say under their right of "freedom of speech" for which they are forever unwilling to offer anything beyond their treasonous rhetoric to safeguard it. God help us if we fail to identify them for what they are, do, and fail to do. Patriotic Americans will defend to death one's God-given right of freedom of speech, but they will not defend one's right to speak or act against the vital interests of the United States of America.

Patriotic Americans seek knowledge of methods, ways, and means of helping to make the United States a stronger, safer, and better nation. One of the keys to succeeding in this noble effort is to promote cohesiveness and unity of effort in business, industry, and the professions. Americans must come to realize that management and labor share a common goal, that what is good for management is also good for labor, that productivity is the key to prosperity, that no one benefits from low productivity and resulting inflation. The substance of a speech that the author made in the 1980s to the Society of Women Executives contains the fundamentals of productivity that both management and labor need to embrace and observe in their day-to-day relations. It appears in this book for that specific reason.

MAXIMIZING AMERICAN PRODUCTIVITY

AN ADDRESS TO THE SOCIETY OF WOMEN EXECUTIVES

"If America is to realize the fullness of her monumental industrial potential, there must be a marriage of management and labor in which their common purpose is identified, understood, and pursued with the totality of their combined energies."

I CAME HERE THIS MORNING TO SPEAK, AND YOU CAME here to listen. I hope you don't finish before I do, but if you do, feel free to leave. I believe, however, that I have some things to say that will be worth your time. Otherwise, I would have turned down the invitation to be here.

One of the enduring national objectives of the United States is to strengthen America's industrial might in order to make life better for every American, regardless of his or her present station in life. Are there not some facts about how to achieve this to which we can all agree and then teach those facts to all of our citizenry? Is there not a common

goal that both management and labor can pursue? Or must
the conflict between management and labor exist eternally?
Why cannot certain fundamental truths concerning productivity, for example, be embraced by working America? I
believe that management and labor share a common goal,
but poor leadership and sometimes lack of knowledge on
the part of the heads of both business and labor perpetu-
ate conflict where harmony should exist. I believe it was
Mahatma Gandhi who said that "We must become the
change we want to see," and if that change is ever to come
about, the nation's executive leadership must lead the way.

Industrial leaders are preoccupied with increased productivity and profit, and they should be. Should not the labor
force be likewise preoccupied? When a company's productivity fails to grow or begins a decline, who is damaged by it?
The answer is, of course, both the company and its employees,
but the workers will probably be the first to feel its impact.
Layoffs almost always begin at the working level.

All of you here this morning may be outstanding executives, but when comparing yourselves with each other, *half
of you are below average.* I made that statement only to get
your attention, because I want to talk to you about some
things that you, your associates, and your work force really
need to know. Some of you come from companies with
organized labor, and labor unions need to know economics
as much as does management Having said that, let me talk
to you this morning about the one subject that makes or
breaks every executive. That subject is *productivity.* On that
one word rests a lot of things.

Productivity may mean one thing to one executive and

something altogether different to another depending on the type of activity in which the organization is engaged. In some professions, productivity is difficult to measure. After retiring from the Army, I became a development officer at the University of Alabama and a part-time professor in the College of Commerce and Business at that institution. We raised funds, millions of dollars, and we measured productivity in terms of how much money we were able to raise for each dollar we invested in the effort. I really don't know how other university administrators measured their productivity. I sometimes make a joke of saying that if one took a hundred university administrators, gave each of them a secretary, and put them in some building but gave them no mission whatsoever, within three months they would have a paperwork backlog and be cranking out requests to upgrade their positions.

I won't be dwelling this morning on that type of activity. I'll be talking about something we can measure, and I'll define it as Webster does. *Productivity is a measure of how efficiently goods and services are produced.*

In most instances, a manager would want to measure productivity in output per employee hour—that is to say some number divided by the number of man-hours worked. For example, let's suppose that a sawmill with a crew of 10 is producing an average of 8,000 board feet of green lumber daily. Assuming that the work day is eight hours, productivity would therefore be 100 (8,000 divided by the man-hour total of 80). The owner has noticed, however, that the blocksetter is too slow in responding to the sawyer's instructions, and the sawyer himself is sometimes unsure of the settings he should give to the blocksetter. The thirders are taking too much time in turning the logs. The lumber and slab handlers are not well coordinated, and the timber cutters are not always making good judgments as to the length that logs of a particular diameter should be cut.

The owner decides that he will devote one full 8-hour day to a training program for his employees. The result is a daily increase of 4,000 board feet. Productivity has therefore increased by 50 percent. The 8-hour training period will pay for itself in a 2-day period.

Let's further say that after granting an across-the-board pay raise the owner utilizes the remainder of his additional revenues to purchase more modern equipment, and once it is in place and operating, the average daily output increases another 4,000 board feet per day. Productivity is now 200 board feet per hour. Now, if the owner can successfully market the timber, all is rosy. But what happens if there is no market for the lumber. The answer is obvious: He shuts down the sawmill, and 10 people are out of work. So is the owner. The lesson here is that a manufacturer of the supplies ought to know the extent of the demand, and if he or she doesn't know that, disaster could well await both management and labor. When demand drops below the ability to produce, the smart executive will be looking toward diversification. Otherwise, fewer jobs will exist.

I was looking at some figures recently that tracked national productivity from 1945 to 1980, a period of 35 years spanning the presidencies of Harry Truman (8 years), Dwight Eisenhower (8 years), John F. Kennedy (2 years), Lyndon Johnson (6 years), Richard Nixon (5-plus years),

Gerald Ford (2-plus years), and Jimmy Carter (four years). Productivity increased on a national scale by 3.0 percent per year from 1945 until we got into the Vietnam War in 1965. During the next eight years, the growth rate dropped to 2.3 percent per year. During the next five years, productivity dropped to a 1.0 percent per year increase, and it actually declined since that time. The decline was about 1.0 percent in 1979 and almost 2.0 percent in 1980.

The decline had very serious implications: First of all, the decline affected our standard of living. Workers had less money, because income rises and falls with output. The production of more goods generates more wage, salary, and dividend income to buy the increased output. As an example, the average American family would have had over $5,000 more income in 1980 than it did have—if the 3.0 percent annual growth rate had continued after 1965.

A decline in productivity is the prime cause of inflation. The inflation rate rose to over 20-percent under Jimmy Carter's watch. Workers needed more money, because they had less buying power. In fact, we can use 1980 to explain how things invariably happen. Suppose that the workers in a particular company threaten to strike if the company does not meet their demands for a 5.0 percent wage increase. In 1980, however, the company's productivity declined by 2.0 percent and the outlook for 1981 indicates that productivity will remain the same. If to prevent a strike, the company grants the 5.0 percent pay raise, its labor costs will rise 7.0 percent (5.0 plus 2.0 percent decline in productivity). The company will simply pass that cost on to the consumer by increasing the per item cost. The 5.0 percent increase that the workers received will not be a real increase at all but in fact a decrease of 2.0 percent. This usually results in demands for a further wage increase. This is called the well-familiar "wage price spiral." Many companies hike their prices to be able to have enough money to modernize their machinery and equipment,, and in these cases, the inflation rate is compounded. If the work force had understood all of these economics, would they have given the company such an ultimatum? In the presence of good executive leadership, where employees are being trained to advance up the ladder of success and become executives themselves, the answer is NO.

Americans everywhere should be aware of the causes of productivity decline. A major cause *is* a decrease in the construction of new factories and the acquisition of better production equipment and machinery. A business can have the best work force in the world, but worker effort and efficiency can't offset the problems associated with poor machinery and low-quality equipment. It is in the best interest of both management and labor that adequate revenues exist for the acquisition of modern machinery and equipment. Productivity can suffer also when inadequate funds are invested in research and development (R&D). During the Carter Administration, America invested less money in R&D, and consequently the nation's businesses have less new machinery and older factory equipment. This is what happened to Gulf States Paper Corporation at its mill in Tuscaloosa, Alabama. The machinery had grown old and inefficient, and the mill was losing in excess of $2 million annually. Even so, the owner and Chief Executive Officer, Jack Warner, didn't want to shut down the mill, knowing what it would do to his employees and the economy of Tuscaloosa. Yet, the workers refused to agree to a contract that offered more but which would cause Gulf States Paper Corporation to suffer an even greater annual loss. They wanted more than the company could pay, and Mr. Warner opted to close the factory. When he announced the decision, the workers decided to accept the contract that they had previously rejected, but it was too late. Mr. Warner's decision was final, and it should have been. Labor had failed to understand their role in the successful operation of Gulf States Paper Corporation, and they suffered the consequences.

Excessive government regulation in the environmental and safety areas has an adverse impact on productivity. I don't believe that the impact is quite as great as the slowdown in the development of technology, but the impact is great enough to be significant. Go examine the figures and talk to the people who are having to abide by one restriction or rule after another, and you'll learn that industrial costs are being driven upward by these regulations. And in many instances the ones being hurt the most are the ones the regulations seek to protect. I meet and talk to a lot of business people about making significant charitable contributions to the University of Alabama. Invariably, they speak of the need to invest in better machinery and equipment but seldom miss mentioning the need to rid themselves of the ball and chains that government regulations place around their ankles.

I am not saying that all government regulation is bad. Some is good, but it doesn't stand to reason that the White House Staff must now be 1,500 strong when President

Roosevelt was able to lead us through World War II with a staff of 40. I would think that a truly objective analysis of the true needs of the country would result in a significant decrease in the number of persons now employed in the various governmental operations in Washington, D.C. A lot of things going on in Washington are related to each other and would be more effective if consolidated, but that just isn't likely to happen very often in our capital city. I did play a part in creating one new organization myself. While a manpower officer with the Joint Chiefs of Staff, we organized the Defense Mapping Agency by consolidating the cartography and geodetic survey functions of the Army, Navy, and Air Force into a single organization, reduced total manpower substantially, improved proficiency, and saved a lot of money.

The tendency among Washington lawmakers and bureaucrats is always to regulate, to increase the work force, and put more power in the hands of government—but in most instances the regulations are imposed without proper analysis of the total impact. In many more instances than not, the regulations cripple free enterprise and stagnate American ingenuity and productivity. The market forces simply aren't permitted to work.

The question is: What do we do? First of all, we have to find a way to bury the perception that stimulating business investment is a criminal act against the poor. In order to get elected, we hear the all-too-familiar chant that the "rich get richer, and the poor get poorer," but there is no way to help the poor except by the creation of jobs that pay a living wage.

Business investments aren't going to be made in the presence of low corporate profits, inflation, and high taxation. As we sit here in this auditorium this morning, after-tax profits for our non-financial corporations continue to drop, and they've been dropping for the past three years. And what has caused it? *The answer is declining productivity and reduced investment and inflation that result from it. . One is compounded by the other. On one hand, falling productivity contributes to inflation. Inflation discourages investment, and declining investment contributes to falling productivity.* Can't we educate Americans everywhere to those simple economic facts and rid every level of government of politicians who deny these fundamental truths just to get elected? I honestly believe that some politicians want to keep the poor people poor, so they can prey upon their hardship to gain their vote.

We have our own selves to blame for letting inflation run as rampant as it did during the Jimmy Carter administration. *Our* national leadership stood by and watched inflation increase effective tax rates on corporate profits, as opposed to the stated tax rates. The stated tax rates on corporate profits increased, because the taxable profits included superficial gains from the inflated value of inventories—and from underestimating plant and equipment replacement costs. Our industrial corporations are no different in this respect from an individual whose taxes go up because his salary increases, but the value of the dollar declines.

Not a one of us here this morning may hold a Ph.D. in Economics, but I think we've seen enough of what's going on in this country to cause us to carry a message to our senators and congressmen that the only way they're going to get our vote is to begin right now to enact legislation that will abolish all government regulation except that which is absolutely mandatory. Let's demand of them that they give Americans free rein where the forces of the market can dictate supply and demand. Trust us to be able to sort out what's good and bad. We don't need some politician to tell us that something is bad, and we don't need some environmental kook to tell us that a paper mill stinks or that a snail darter lives in water.

Finally, let me ask each of you again to hear me out on this one point. We need a massive education program for Democrats, Republicans, Independents, and any others that may come along. The American people, all of us, must be shown that controlling inflation and spurring productivity can only be done by rewarding investment, technological advancement, research and development, modernization of equipment, keeping taxes to a bare minimum, and removing the restrictive regulations that have placed a ball and chain on productivity. We need to expose the motives of those who oppose industrial growth and prey on the poor with such statements as "the rich get richer and the poor get poorer." Politicians have played on the ignorance of some and insulted the intelligence of others with this over-used hogwash, and it's time for them to come to know that they cannot continue keeping people poor in order to hold political power. Our political leaders must learn to put America first. If something is harmful to productivity, it is harmful to the American people, and no politician should embrace something harmful without suffering a day of reckoning at the ballot box.

If America is to maintain its dominant position in the world, we must outperform the people of other nations. In the military, we tell our young soldiers what we're going to tell them. We tell them, and then we tell them what we told them. Even then, we often have to repeat the process. Eventually, they do things better than their civilian counterparts. Now, this is not to say that we should militarize America—far from it. What I'm saying is that we should educate the American workforce on what is good and bad for America, give them the best on-the-job training that the world has ever known, and thereby enable them to advance to the level of their incompetence. Every American has that God-given right, and every executive in America should see that it happens. Once that kind of leadership permeates business and industry, conflicts between management and labor will cease, and productivity will reach levels that we never imagined.

Thank you for inviting me here today. I wish you well in what you do, and I ask you to include my name among those who believe in *equal pay for equal work*. Women haven't achieved that yet, but the time is coming.

Several years ago, I was selected as the Honorary Colonel of the 58th Infantry Regiment, a honorary position I continue to hold. With so many former officers of the regiment to select from, I was humbled by the act of the Secretary of the Army and the Chief of Infantry to honor me in such a way. I have since spent many days at Fort Benning, Georgia, addressing the officers and men of the 58th Infantry "Patriots," a name I gave to the regiment during the Vietnam War. Like the foregoing address to the Society of Women Executives, I have a purpose for including one of my addresses to the 58th Infantry and to members of their families invited to a ceremonial parade at the end of a training cycle. That purpose is to underscore the need for America to approach every undertaking as if human life is up for grabs. We can learn to do that by studying the ways of the soldier.

A Message to New Infantrymen and Their Families

*There they go—the doggies, the doughboys, the footsloggers,
the Queen of Battle. God bless them! I love them!*

—Ernie Pyle, 1944

I WANT TO EXPRESS MY MOST PROFOUND GRATITUDE TO all of you special people who have gathered here this morning—grandfathers and grandmothers, parents, spouses, loved ones, and friends—who have braved the weather and in most cases traveled hundreds of miles to help honor the great young men of the 58th Infantry who this day proudly don the blue of dogface soldier. Don't these young Infantrymen look good in their dress uniforms with the blue cords on their shoulder, the National Defense Service Ribbon on their chests, and with haircuts befitting the soldier? They arrived

IRON MIKE –
SYMBOL OF INFANTRY

at Fort Benning five months ago with long flowing locks that gathered dust, microbes, and a myriad of other foreign particles of questionable value. Now look at them! They make me proud to be their Honorary Colonel.

They look pristine and immaculate, but the way they appear this morning is light years from what they normally are. You are looking at the "doughboy," the "doggie," the "dogface," the "footslogger," the "Queen of Battle." When the battle is joined, the dogface soldiers lined up across this parade field will be the first to be there—nose-to-nose, eyeball-to-eyeball, guts-to-guts, blood-to-blood, and mud-to-mud. And it's always the same mud and the same blood. When wars come along, two things happen immediately. First, the devil increases the size of hell. Then, some terrestrial force moves the mud from one land mass to another for the soldier to wade through. It's a special type of mud that sticks to the combat boots like no other mud on Planet Earth. Everyone of you old soldiers gathered here today know exactly what I'm talking about.

You wonderful people who love the soldier enough to be here are looking at the elite of the Army and the best young men America has to offer. The dogface soldier is always in the lead and the forward-most point of contact. Everything revolves around him. He is the basic instrument of war and the noblest of all of the things that God has created.

It is appointed for others to sit in the seats of government and to turn the wheels of business and industry, but it is cast the lot of the soldier to lay down his life for his country. If the Chief Executive Officer of a company fails, the business fails, but if the Infantryman fails in his job, the nation will fall. Therein lies the fundamental differ-ence between the soldier and all other Americans. He is the nation's true patriot, because he stands ready to give his life for his country. He enables others to make millions for doing safe things or even for playing games, but he is paid a starvation wage, while standing in the face of an enemy who is seeking to take his life. The Creator of this world said that "Greater love hath no man than this . . ."

I want also this morning to express my gratitude to the Drill Sergeants who have taken these great men through their Infantry training. You parents here today may think that you have taught your sons well—that you have been good teachers. I'm sure you have, but these Drill Sergeants have been able to teach your sons a few things with which you may have had difficulty. These young men standing before you have learned to say "yes sir" and "no sir" and "yes ma'am" and "no ma'am." They make up their beds everyday. They clean up their rooms everyday. They hang their clothes up when they take them off or put them in a laundry bag. They even know how to do the dishes. Moreover, they clean up the yard everyday.

Now, in the course of all of this, the Drill Sergeants have taught your sons how to be good teachers themselves. In fact, they have become the most outstanding teachers in the world today. The tyrants on this earth like Saddam Hus-sein just don't listen very well to the diplomats. Diplomacy, economic sanctions, and a whole host of other initiatives just don't penetrate their gray matter. It takes the American soldier to teach them that they are going to pay a monu-mental price for attempting to establish their own international law or for trying to take the freedom of a defenseless neighbor. The man behind the M-16 simply has a better way of explaining things.

I wish I could promise you family members gathered here this morning that the special young men standing before you will never have to taste the horrors of war. I can't do that, because it just seems that wars are a part of the order of things, and no generation of Americans has avoided one. For those of you who believe in the Scriptures, you'll find no difficulty in believing that *war is sometimes instituted by God Himself as a drastic medicine for ailing humanity.* God punished Israel that very way for their disobedience, and He is the same God that He's always been. The only things that are as certain as death and taxes are wars and more wars. *Eternal peace lasts only until the next war,* and being unprepared to fight the next war is cold blooded murder.

You fine young soldiers can't do a thing about the size of the Army or the level of support that you'll receive, but you can be a part of the best small army in the history of the world. I believe you will be. I've looked at you and know your ability. I also know that you have the best weapons and equipment in the world, and I know you serve the greatest nation to ever exist upon the earth. All of this, I know, but I have to say to you this morning that the future fate of this nation will not be determined by money, machinery, technology, or mere mass of numbers. Our future fate, as in the past, will be determined by the deeds of this nation's truest patriots—our soldiers.

Some 30-plus years ago when I gave the name of "Patriots" to the 58th Infantry Regiment, I did it primarily to honor the soldiers who were serving under me. Those men in the regiment at that time were fine soldiers, and the name of "Patriots" fit them well. Yet, the thought occurs to me this morning that the same name fits you fine soldiers even more. You see, there is a great difference between love-of-country and patriotism. What adds so much to the high respect, esteem, and feeling I have for each of you is the knowledge of what a true patriot really is. You meet the definition. *It's only when one's love-of-country becomes strong enough to compel him to voluntarily participate in his country's causes that love-of-country becomes patriotism.* Then, and only then, does one become a patriot. Each one of you is a volunteer. You can rightfully call yourself a patriot, and no one can ever take that away. You've earned it with your deeds.

You have cause to take pride in what you have done here at Fort Benning. You have been challenged and proved that you have what it takes. You now wear the blue cord of the Infantry. Everything that has happened here has been a part of your training and preparation, and thus far, you have measured up. But now, you enter into a new phase. Your service to the Army and the nation begins today. It's now your time at bat, and as you walk up to the plate, you have been handed a monumental responsibility and a great tradition to uphold.

As you leave here and go to your places of duty, lend an ear to the voices of those who have gone on before you. Some voices will be coming from Flanders Field, Arlington National Cemetery, and from under white crosses and unmarked graves around the world. I want to believe that from somewhere they are watching and saying "Don't let us down! We gave you what you've got. Keep it for those who follow you. Don't let us down!"

The night before the Normandy Invasion in 1944, General Eisenhower remarked to his soldiers that "The eyes of the world are upon you." Now, the eyes of the world are watching you again, and if the tyrant ever sees any weakness that would cause him to believe that he can beat you, you can be sure that he will try. If he ever believes that you lack the will to fight, he'll set out to achieve his ends by both blackmail and open warfare. The end result could well be the decline and eventual demise of the United States. As ominous as that statement may sound, it could well happen, and the sands of time are strewn with the bones of those who never thought that such could happen to nations thought invincible.

Throughout history, great nations and great civilizations have fallen, because the people of those nations lost the will to fight, the desire for self-sacrifice, or the necessary dedication to their country and the way of life it represented. The very ultimate in the ideals of patriotism, honor, duty, sacrifice, and respect for tradition must exist in the hearts and minds of every American soldier. I look at you great young men standing here this morning, and I will leave Fort Benning this day knowing that "The Land of the Free and the Home of the Brave" will continue to be "The Land of the Free and the Home of the Brave." I look in your eyes, and I see a spirit that has kept the nation free for over eleven score years. You must never falter or let that spirit die. The destiny of the United States rests upon it.

I am an Infantryman by choice and an Infantryman

by nature, and so it's easy for me to love and respect the dogface soldier. You are the best thing America owns, and I honor you and salute you. You have my solemn promise that I will pray that God will always give you a generous helping of courage and walk beside you in all that you do.

It would be a miscarriage of justice if this book failed to mention the wives and children of our servicemen. It is true that no profession on earth tests the mettle of mankind as much as does the honorable profession of arms, but there is also no people on earth who pay a greater price than does the soldier's wife and children. They are no better prepared physically, mentally, or emotionally to withstand the physical hardships they endure or the mental and emotional trauma with which they are so frequently faced. Their lives are fraught with trials, tribulations, and abuse that is sometimes directed at them by their own countrymen. In times of war, their day is spent in limbo, never knowing whether the dreaded notification of the next of kin will be delivered to their door. The abbreviated bio that follows relates some of the experiences of Jane O'Mary and our children during 25 of my 32 years of Army service. More, much more, happened to them, but for those who have never been there and done that, the part of the story that I have recorded is enough to let one know that the soldier's wife has earned her keep. There's a more compelling reason, however, for including this narrative in God and Country Forever. It carries a message that all Americans have a role to play in keeping our nation free.

War, Peace, and the Army Wife

"To the Army wife, even a time of peace is war in masquerade."

JANE MARIE, THE YEAR I MET HER (1950). THE PHOTO I CARRIED IN MY BILLFOLD IN BOTH KOREA AND VIETNAM.

Her maiden name was Jane Marie Murphree, and she was the most stunningly beautiful girl that I had ever seen. She was 18 years old, and I was 24 the day I first saw her. She was standing in front of her college dormitory with several other girls, but she was so strikingly resplendent that the others faded into oblivion. I was a ROTC cadet, working hard to acquire a Regular Army Commission and was hurrying to a meeting with the Professor of Military Science and Tactics, but I found myself just standing and staring from a sidewalk across the street. Had the time been available, I don't think I would have had the nerve to walk over and speak. I would have to figure out a perfect way, I thought, to meet her—one that would not turn her away.

So, I went on over to the meeting and said to my lifetime friend, Cadet Major (later Army Lieutenant Colonel) O.J. (Sam) Hyde, that "I have just seen the Goddess of Beauty, and she's a student here on this campus." He asked me who she was, and I said that "I don't know, but she puts Aphrodite out of business." I remember well his saying, "Go get her before somebody else does," and from that moment on, I never dated another girl. I changed her name from Murphree to O'Mary on 8 July 1951, a year before graduating.

The only material thing we owned was a 1937 Pontiac that wouldn't go into reverse gear. Fortunately, I had already served a tour in the Army, benefited from the GI Bill, and also had an athletic scholarship that paid $35 per month. Married veterans were given priority over students for campus housing at a place called "Splinter Village." Each little house had one single bed (3-feet wide), a two-eyed gas stove, an icebox, one small kitchen table, a sofa, and a pot-bellied stove that burned wood and coal to heat the little place. Build a fire and be too hot or let it die down and freeze half to death. Not having enough money to keep the icebox supplied with ice, the alternative course of action was to open a window and put stuff on the ledge. Unable to pay the remaining expenses for the two of us to attend college, we found no other option except for my precious beautiful bride to drop out of school and go to work at a small eating place frequented by classmates and friends. It was humiliating to her, painful for her parents, who were all college graduates, and there is no way to express the impact it continues to have on me 52 years later. I will always feel remorseful for asking her to marry me before I had the means to support her and subject her to such an experience. I thought I might lose her if I didn't, but that is no justification for expecting to ever be forgiven by either God or man. I just loved her so deeply, and there is nothing I wouldn't do to keep her. I kept trying to justify my actions by telling myself that I would be going in the Army at the end of her sophomore year, and she couldn't marry me anyway without dropping out of college.

The last five months of 1951 and the first four months of 1952 were the longest ones I can remember, but graduation day finally arrived. I was fortunate enough to graduate with honors and receive a Regular Army commission. Happy days had come at last when I received my diploma and was concurrently notified by the Army that I was to realize my life-long dream of being an Infantry officer. The Army's orders assigned me to the 47th Infantry Division at Camp Rucker, Alabama, with temporary duty enroute to Fort Benning, Georgia, where I was to attend a 22-week Basic Infantry Course—unaccompanied by dependents. The reporting date was 14 June, but upon arrival, I learned that the Army orders should have placed me on leave at my home of record without pay and allowance status until the start of the class on 23 August. However, since I had previously been a Non-Commissioned Officer (NCO) in the Army, the Infantry School at Fort Benning took advantage of my availability and assigned me as a Tactical Officer for an NCO Leadership Course, pending the start of my own class.

My work day started about 5:00 A.M. and ended about 10:30 P.M. Saturday afternoons and Sundays belonged to me, and I would use that time to spend with Jane, now living with her parents at Fairfax, Alabama (Jane had helped them move from Arley, Alabama). Her father had accepted a position as Superintendent of Fairfax Valley High School. We were most fortunate, because the distance was less than 50 miles. In order to get there, however, I needed a car, having disposed of my 1937 Pontiac to an automobile junkyard dealer for a whopping price of $50. I had no money for a down-payment, but by offering an extra $100 above the asking price and agreeing to pay for it in one year; I drove away with a 1949 Plymouth. It was on the second Sunday we spent together in Fairfax that we joined a local Baptist Church, a pattern of speedy church-joining that we have followed all of our married life.

Fortunately, newly commissioned officers received an initial uniform allowance that one took to the Post Quartermaster Sales Store. The only things they needed to know were head, neck, waist, trouser length, and shoe size. They knew exactly how many of what the money would buy and the minimum needed, and within minutes the items were stacked in front of you—no trying on, no measuring, no tailoring. They took your quarters allowance, and you left. For the rest of your career, clothing purchases were the officer's responsibility—no more allowances. The pay of a brand new Second Lieutenant including allowances was a little over $300, but that was far more than that to which we had been accustomed. I make mention of this initial tour of duty and the pay I received, because it would pose a hardship on my dear Army wife almost two years later— something I'll talk about in a later paragraph.

Upon completing the Basic Course, Jane and I put all of our belongings in the back seat and trunk of our 1949 Plymouth and headed to Camp Rucker, Alabama, a couple of days before my reporting date. There was no post housing, and neither were there any vacant furnished apartments in the nearby towns of Ozark and Enterprise, but as luck would have it, someone told us of a furnished apartment in Dothan, Alabama, owned by "Rip" Hughes, long time head coach of the Dothan High School football team. The distance was 30 miles, but we wasted no time in getting there. We arrived in the nick of time, beating another couple by only a matter of minutes, and told Coach Hughes we'd take it. Looking back upon it, the place wasn't much, but we didn't know it. We were just happy to have a place to live, and it didn't seem to matter that I had to get up at 4:00 AM every morning, drive to Camp Rucker, help prepare a company of soldiers to fight in Korea, and on most days leave for Dothan at nightfall. Jane and I didn't have much time together, but treasured the fleeting moments we shared.

Less than three months after arriving at Camp Rucker, orders came assigning me to Korea. The time had come for me to find out if I could measure up. I had become an Infantryman by choice. Now I would learn if I was also an Infantryman by nature. All of my training and my thoughts had been focused on leading men in combat. I had given little thought to getting killed or how to leave a precious and wonderful wife who meant more to me than life itself. The toughest thing I've ever had to do was to tell Jane goodbye, not knowing when or if I would ever see her again. I can't remember the last words I said, but I know that every cell in my body ached, trembled, and wept. Three days later, I found myself in the 3rd Battalion, 65th Infantry near Kumhwa, South Korea, doing the things that I had prepared myself physically, mentally, and emotionally to do. As young Army wives must sometimes do, Jane went home to live with her parents again and took a job—in part to free her mind of the war for a few moments during the day but to also help meet the nine more payments we had left on our 49 Plymouth.

Mail call is something that all soldiers look forward to, particularly in combat. Near the end of the war, we had just completed fighting a tremendous battle in the Iron Triangle, referred to later as the "Kumsong River Salient," a vignette about which I have included in this book. It hadn't been possible to deliver us any mail for a couple of weeks, and when the mail finally did arrive, the amount was unusually large. Mixed among several letters I had received from Jane was a piece of correspondence from the Comptroller General of the Army, and its substance was not heartwarming. It was an information copy of a letter addressed to our Finance Officer at Fort Rucker stating that I was not entitled to be paid for my service as a Tactical Officer at Fort Benning, Georgia, from 14 June to 23 August 1952 and to reclaim the money immediately. The amount they said I owed was $693, as best I recall—not a large amount in 2006 but a lot of money in 1953.

I think I would have been just as mad if the amount had been $10. I had worked over 12 hours a day, wore the uniform, and was subject to Courts-Martial. Yet, the Comptroller General of the Army said I shouldn't be paid.

I didn't carry around a typewriter in combat and had no means of responding in the normal way. I instead wrote a note on a piece of paper and sent it back to our Personnel Officer, telling him the essentials of the matter and asking him to request of the Finance Officer that the collection action be delayed until the situation enabled me to formally state my case. To make a long story short, the note worked. I heard no more about it and continued to be paid during my remaining time in Korea. By no means, however, was the Comptroller General's directive forgotten—certainly not by the Comptroller.

When I had finished serving a year and half in Korea, I was reassigned to the Infantry School at Fort Benning, Georgia. I didn't know what I would be teaching there, but I was elated. Fort Benning is the home of the Infantry, and to be assigned to the Infantry School as an Instructor seemed too good to be true. Instructors are sent through "Charm School," and every class one attends there is a Cecil B. de Mille production, and I would now be a part of it. So, after spending three wonderful weeks with Jane, we traveled to Fort Benning to again search for a place to live. There being no on-post housing available for First Lieutenants (I had been promoted in Korea), we rented a small furnished house about two miles from the post, and a few days later I reported for duty.

Someone in my career branch in the Pentagon had talked to the Infantry School about me prior to my arrival, and a message was waiting for me when I signed in telling me to call the Infantry School's Personnel Department Director's Office as soon as I arrived. The person manning the desk dialed the office and handed me the phone. I was told by the person on the other end that the Department Director wanted to talk to me and to call back that afternoon for a time and place. I well remember reporting to the Director's office at 0800 (8:00 A.M.) the following morning with a new haircut, spit-polished boots, brass shined—looking as sharp as I possibly could. I was greeted by the Department Director who introduced me to Lieutenant Colonel Robert J. McDonald, a tall, robust impressive man who was wearing more decorations on his chest than I had ever seen. I noticed the 101st Airborne Division patch on his right shoulder and concluded that he had been with General McAuliffe at Bastogne. Both he and the Department Director shook my hand, welcomed me to the Infantry School, and invited me to take a seat. Until that moment, I had been standing as stiff as a board. The Director immediately got down to business by telling me that Colonel McDonald (all Lieutenant Colonels are addressed as Colonel) was the Chairman of the Leadership Committee and wanted to ask me some questions. Colonel McDonald had some papers in front of him and after looking down at them for a moment said to me, "Lieutenant O'Mary, Infantry Branch tells me that you were a pretty damn good company commander in Korea and tough as nails. Just how tough were you?" To this day, I don't know what prompted me to respond the way I did, but smiling back at him, I said, "Sir, for anyone to be tougher than I was, they would have had to be born out of wedlock and murdered their own mother." Both of them roared with laughter, and Colonel McDonald looked at the Department Director and said, "I think we've got our man." The questioning was over about as fast as it started.

A few minutes later, I would be taken by my new boss and introduced to the other members of the Leadership Committee, Captains and above, who were among the most highly-decorated and esteemed officers in the Army. I was to be the only Lieutenant on the committee, and provided I could pass "Charm School," it would be my responsibility to teach officer candidates (ocs) and Second Lieutenants fresh out of college how to lead other men.

Several things had to be done that afternoon—getting post tags for the car, buying more uniforms including khaki shorts and a pith helmet, and delivering my pay record to Post Finance, where I had hoped to get a couple of hundred dollars of advance pay. There I received the heartwarming news that the Comptroller General had directed the Finance Officer to collect the $693 of "unauthorized pay" that I received in July and August of 1952—that such reclaim action could be spread over a 90-day period, if I so elected, "to prevent undue hardship." Taking the glad tidings home to Jane was not the most enjoyable event I can remember. Breaking the news brought her to tears—no screams, just tears and silence. Then, after a few moments, she said, "Paul, I'll have to find a job tomorrow. We can't keep this house and eat if I don't." I knew she was right, but it hurt so awful much. I thought about what I had put her through in the three years of our marriage, and it just destroyed every smidgeon of personal pride I owned.

We had only the one car and reasoned that finding a job on the post would enable us to drive to work together.

Almost as if the Lord planned it, we learned that the Officers Club Receptionist had quit her job that very day. Jane
applied for the job, and the Club Officer hired her without
looking further. Who wouldn't hire someone with half her
looks and talent? The job paid enough to get us through
the following three months while I paid back the $693 that
the Comptroller said I owed. It was not the type of job that
anyone would enjoy, but a higher-paying job lay in wait.

The wife of one of our newly-acquired friends told Jane
of an opening for an inventory clerk at the Book Store, a
very large retail store on post that handled a wide variety
of goods. Books could be purchased there, but so could a
wide assortment of merchandise—- all kinds of military
uniform paraphernalia and household items of every sort
and kind, including kitchen appliances, washers and dryers,
televisions, radios, whatever. If the Book Store didn't have
it, the manager (an Army Major) would order it wholesale
and sell it to the buyer at a price he determined. Profits
from the Book Store sales were transferred to the Central
Post Fund to be used for the health, education, and welfare
of the troops on post. Jane applied for the job, and Major X
hired her immediately and in less than a month promoted
her to Stock Control Manager and made her accountable
for all of the stock on hand—worth hundreds of thousands
of dollars.

Being accountable was not something Jane couldn't
handle. What did trouble her was the periodic inquiries of
Major X over a period of several months as to the number of some item or items on hand. She would give him a
number from the Inventory Account, and he would invari-

ably say something like "I thought we had that many, too, but I can't find them or I can't find but a certain number." After a series of the Major's inquiries about items that were always short and never an inquiry about any item in which the number on the inventory account matched the number on hand, Jane became deeply troubled and broke the news to me. We needed the money, but Jane and I decided that walking away from that job a week earlier would have been too late. Inasmuch as she was pregnant with our first child and suffering from morning sickness, it was convenient for her to tender her resignation "for personal reasons."

I knew God was watching when two days later we were informed by Post Housing that a small unfurnished apartment (about 700 square feet) had become vacant on post. We needed furniture and bought only those items that were absolutely necessary and the cheapest we could find—almost exclusively unfinished items that we could stain and varnish. The only luxury item in that little place was a 17-inch black and white Capehart Television. Color television had not yet arrived on the scene.

Several months later, news of an investigation into the activities of Major X hit the local media. Relating all of what the investigation turned up would require volumes and is beyond the scope of this abbreviated biography. A mention of it is necessary, however, to show how Jane's judgment, integrity, and God's watchful eye saved her from being caught up in a scandal that ended the career of an Army Major. Moreover, we could now look forward to the birth of our first child, having paid back the money that the Comptroller General said I wasn't authorized to receive.

In those days, the Army didn't reduce one's taxable income by an amount that may have been reclaimed. Jane and I paid Federal and State taxes on the money when I first earned it in 1952, and I paid taxes on it again when I paid it back in 1954. When I was preparing my income tax return for 1954, I listed the money as a deduction, but the IRS didn't allow it, officially ruling that the loss would have had to be declared on my 1953 return—an arbitrary judgment by some self-appointed genius that I never viewed as right and just. The comedy, however, doesn't end here. In 1956, the Comptroller General ruled that I was entitled to the money after all, and I kissed that green card when it arrived. The amount, however, was added to my total income, and Jane and I paid Federal and State taxes on the same $693 for the third time in four years.

Everything was different back then. At about 4:00 A.M. on the morning of 28 May 1956, Jane began experiencing labor pains, and it was off to the Fort Benning Hospital. Upon arrival, some guy came out with a wheel chair, told me that they would notify me when the baby was born, and carted Jane away. I heard nothing from anybody until late in the afternoon of 29 May, when a woman called from the hospital telling me that the baby had been born. I asked if it was OK, if Jane was OK, and if it was a boy or a girl. The woman said that "Your wife will tell you about that when you get here. You can visit her for a short time." When I got there, I learned that Jane was OK and Mary O'Mary was OK—the most beautiful mother and baby I had ever seen.

I would complete my tour with the Leadership Committee a year later, attend the 10-months long Infantry Officer Advanced Course, where Jane and I would meet our long-time great friends, Bob and Pat Hurley. The odds of its happening would be infinitely small, but Bob and I would from that time on serve at the same locations for 10

BOB & PAT HURLEY

years in the Third Infantry (The Old Guard) at Fort Myer, Virginia, the Command and General Staff College at Fort Leavenworth, Kansas, in Berlin during the building of the wall, in the Pentagon, and Vietnam. We laughed together, shared some trying moments together, and gave things our best shot. Bob's and Pat's deep friendship continues to rest among the rewards of service to country that Jane and I treasure more than life.

It was a high honor to be selected for duty in the Old Guard (the President's Own). Everyone had to be between 5'11" and 6' 2", be able to march flawlessly, and have the heart and soul of a determined and dedicated soldier. Private soldiers were carefully screened at the basic training centers, tested for their soldierly skills, and scrutinized for their attitude and moral character. A few of those who measured up in every way would be selected for the Old Guard. It was quite a privilege to command them.

Ike was President and Nixon was Vice President, and our mission brought us in close contact with them. Having command of a 350-man company that inter alia included a Saluting Battery (3-inch guns) as well as the Army's last remaining horses and caissons, I shared in the responsibility for all full-honor burials in Arlington National Cemetery, interring such noted men as Fleet Admirals William Leahy and "Bull" Halsey, "Flying Tiger" Lee Chennault, and former Secretary of State John Foster Dulles among 25 funerals being conducted daily. With exception of General of the Army George C. Marshall, all general officers and admirals were interred with full honors—horse-drawn caisson, 21 guns, and marching platoons from the Army, Navy, Air Force, and Marines. He had asked to be interred as a simple soldier, and Mrs. Marshall saw to it that his wish was granted. Thousands of dignitaries from across America and around the world gathered near the gates of the cemetery that day, but my dear friend and comrade, First Lieutenant (later Colonel) Dick Barrere did his job as all good soldiers do. He sealed the entrances to Arlington Cemetery, permitting the Marshall family to hold their private ceremony with no others present, except the buglers and a seven-man firing party.

The rules of protocol provided that every chief-of-state visiting the United States be honored at the airport with a 21-gun salute, escorted by the President or Vice President to a point in front of the Blair House, where a red carpet had been spread upon the walkway from the street to the steps. Certain officers in the Old Guard were selected as aides to the President and Vice President, and among other things it was their responsibility to be present at the Pan American Building on the evening of the date of a chief-of-state's arrival to assist Vice President Nixon in hosting the dinner. It was an awesome experience for a young Army officer (now a captain) from the backwoods of Alabama to be able to meet and dine with kings, presidents, prime ministers, premiers, members of the Supreme Court such as Chief Justice Earl Warren and Justice Hugo Black, and many other renowned Americans invited as guests. Jane never attended any of these, but I was able on one occasion to take the head table centerpiece home to her. It was so big we didn't have any place to put it, but it was nevertheless a fitting honor to an Army wife.

Among other experiences, my company was given full protocol and logistical responsibility for the visit of Nikita Kruschev and the 280-strong contingent accompanying him. Some of us didn't sleep in a bed for the entire time the blusterous old Communist was in country. The State Department seemed to go into hiding and turned everything over to us, and I'll never forget the demands I had to place on my Executive Officer and Tank Platoon Leader, First Lieutenant (later Colonel) Cecil G. (Bud) Fair and the men he led. For two weeks, I took him away from his Army wife. They showed a group of Russians how great soldiers look and act.

The Third Infantry conducted at least two parades weekly, honoring dignitaries and high ranking military retirees, commemorating events, or just parading for no good reason. I remember parading in honor of the Russian Attache and, believe it or not, on one occasion we paraded in honor of the Four-Cent Stamp.

All of our activities were by no means ceremonial. Each winter, we put our soldiers through a tough training program at Camp A.P. Hill, Virginia, which was terminated by a treacherous 70-mile patrol up the Appalachian Trail and over the Massanutten Mountains into West Virginia. In short, duty there was no picnic, and there was little time available to spend with the family. Most of the time, I wasn't there when Jane needed me.

In late October 1958, a small wooden office building converted to an apartment became vacant at Fort Myer, and Jane and I were able to move on post. My quarters allowance stopped, but so did the monthly gas, electricity, water, and sewage bills. I could walk to work, leave home later, come home for lunch, live next door to Army friends, and get home earlier. I don't think the convenience had anything to do with it, but Jane told me one day that she was pregnant. We noticed that the load was larger than the one she carried with our first child. Doctors didn't have the technology and know-how that they have today, and it would be into the seventh month before being informed that Jane was carrying twins.

The Third Infantry always held a parade on Sunday afternoon, and one was scheduled for the last Sunday in July of 1959. Jane told me that morning that she believed she may have experienced a labor pain. She said that she felt like something was about to happen, and without thinking clearly, I immediately remarked that "You can't go into labor today. We've got a parade this afternoon, and I have to be there. There's nobody to replace me." Fortunately God and Jane cooperated, and she went into labor immediately after the parade ended. I rushed her to DeWitt Army Hospital at Fort Belvoir, Virginia. Just as they did when our first child was born, the people at the hospital sent me home. After an extremely difficult labor that lasted until late in the afternoon of 1 August, Sharon and Karen O'Mary entered the world from the breach position.

There were many historical and cultural attractions in Washington, D.C. and its environs, but Jane O'Mary would not be able to enjoy them. A three-year old girl and the newly born twins would consume her every waking moment. I helped where and when I could, but for most of the time, I wasn't there when she needed me.

In the spring of 1960, I was notified by the Army that I had been selected to attend the Command and General Staff College at Fort Leavenworth, Kansas, commencing in July of 1960. Once again, it's time to pack up, disassemble the gas range, clean it inside and out, fill in every nail hole where a picture or mirror hung, and in general make the inside look like no one had ever lived there. In the Army, one found it clean and left it clean.

We had leave coming and decided to spend it in Alabama with both of our families. Most of them had not yet seen the twins. When our leave was up, we loaded up the kids in a 57 Plymouth Fury (loved that car) and headed for Leavenworth, Kansas, taking the most direct route through western Tennessee, Arkansas, and Missouri. We were driving through the Arkansas Ozarks on a two-lane road when suddenly a large old truck came down a hill in front of us in our lane, passing several cars on his right and motioning for us to get over. He didn't have to be motioning. I got over as far as I could and came to a full stop with my right wheels less than six inches from the edge of a cliff. His truck hit my left front fender and proceeded on down the left side of my car, taking the door handle with him. The only way we could get out of the car was to open the doors on the passenger side, but the only place to stand was about six feet down. Jane and I helped each other out and were reaching up for the children (we dropped Karen) when this burly guy came running up and said, "I motioned you to get over." I was pretty tough in those days, and I'm glad I didn't have a club in my hands.

We didn't have CBs or cell phones back then, but some good Samaritan offered to call the Arkansas Highway Patrol when he reached the next town. About an hour later, one arrived on the scene. The guy who hit me told the patrolmen that his brake line had broken and that he couldn't stop but that I was to blame. He said that he wouldn't have hit me if I "had moved over as far as I should have." With a set of Virginia tags on my car, I wasn't certain at the moment that justice would come my way in the sovereign State of Arkansas. The patrolmen could see that if I had moved over any further my car would still be rolling. He had a few choice words to say to the nasty old truck driver, directed him to provide me with his name, address, and insurance company. After determining that my car could be driven, the patrolmen wished us well, and we were on our way. After a few days in a body shop in Leavenworth, Kansas, my good old 57 Plymouth looked like new.

Except for the study effort required to do well in a course far tougher than at any civilian institution, the year at the Command and General Staff College would not be one to write home about. Excelling in competition with graduates of West Point, former ROTC Distinguished Military Graduates, and a few Rhodes Scholars thrown in for good measure is a challenge that brings forth a greater effort than one would ordinarily expend. Academic competition brings out one's best, and to those whose minds run along certain channels, the effort itself is exciting.

In the meantime, Jane's at home with the kids in a set of quarters that should have long ago been condemned for human occupancy. Calling the place "quarters" is being overly kind. It was ¼ of an old Army barrack. There were no drawers in the kitchen—just open shelves with no fronts on them that exposed the silverware and dishes to the normal household dust. The washing machine was located in the kitchen and the dryer in one of the bedrooms. An upright post stood in the middle of the living room, requiring a hole to be cut in the middle of our 9 x 12 rug.

The twins neither choose to sleep nor eat at the same time. Jane arises at the first sound from them more than once during the night—not so much because she thinks that I need more sleep than she does but because she's their mother—and the best one to ever walk down the pike. At the end of the school year, the Commandant will declare her a "Gradumate" and bestow upon her a PHT (pushing hubby through), but her honors will end there, and no one except her husband will remember.

A few weeks earlier, we had received good news and bad news from Infantry Branch. The good news was that I was being assigned to Berlin. The Cold War was growing hotter, and that's where the action was. The bad news was that Jane and the kids couldn't go with me. We used the largest part of my leave getting her and the kids moved back to a rented house in Alabama. There was no way to know at the time if we would be separated for a few months, a year, two years, or three years. It was not one of life's happiest moments to leave her and the kids.

Berlin Brigade had already determined what my job would be before I arrived. There was nothing in the Army that I loved more than to serve with dogface soldiers, and I had hoped to be assigned to one of the battle groups. Ordinarily, the idea of being a G-2 or G-3 Operations Officer wouldn't overwhelm me with joy, but in the case of Berlin, there was no better assignment. In the next two and a half years, I would serve in both of those jobs and live the most exciting life outside of actual combat that I have known in the Army. It was tit for tat with the Soviets and East Germans in East Berlin, where we were often boxed in and detained, threatened at gunpoint, headlights kicked out, antennas beaten off of our cars, East Germans voting with their feet and being shot attempting to escape to West Berlin, convoys being detained by the Soviets on the Berlin-Helmstedt Autobahn, U.S. and Soviet tanks confronting each other at Checkpoint Charlie, Soviet busses being over-turned by West Berliners, and others that brought us to the brink of open war.

With those things happening in Berlin, it's still a mystery to me why dependent travel was stopped for all of Europe except Berlin. The reason given was a political and psychological one, but it never made sense to me. As much as I wanted to be with Jane and the kids, I was fearful of bringing them to Berlin. If a war broke out, there would be no sane reason to believe they could make it out from an enclave 110 miles inside East Germany. We had a plan, but the odds of its succeeding added up to minus zero in a thousand chances. The substance of a classified message we received from Washington in late August or early September of 1961, however, convinced me that we were not going to war in the immediate future unless the Soviets forced it on us. The Communist way is to push the bayonet forward until the point strikes steel and then back away. I made the decision that day to bring Jane and the kids to Berlin.

Imagine a woman with two babies and a five-year old with no one to help having to handle all the things that faced Jane at the moment. She had to get our car from Huntsville, Alabama to New Orleans to get it on a ship bound for Bremerhaven, Germany. That left her with no car. She was also restricted on how much she could ship to Berlin (about 3,000 pounds) and what to put in stateside storage. This was in 1961, not 2007, and there was no e-mail or no way to make a telephone call. She could send a telegram with a few words, and that was it. There was no time to write a letter asking for instructions. She was on her own, and as usual, I wasn't there to help.

We had been carrying State Farm Insurance on the car, but that company would not insure a car being driven in a country outside the continental United States. One of their agents, however, sold me a policy with another company (an unfamiliar name that I can't remember now) that provided the overseas coverage. I paid for the first year of coverage, which I was required to do, but that would be a forced mistake, as I will explain later.

Jane followed the Army guidelines as well as she could and on the date specified (in early October 1961) she left by plane from Huntsville, Alabama, with 5-year old Mary and two-year old Sharon and Karen. I had left Berlin the night before on what we called the "Duty Train" from Berlin to Frankfurt, West Germany, where I was met by an Army buddy and driven to his quarters near Heidelberg. The plan called for us to meet Jane's plane at the airport in Frankfurt the following day. It didn't happen that way.

When Jane arrived at McGuire Air Force Base, expecting to depart on the plane I was to meet, she learned that a higher-priority passenger had "bumped" her from her flight. She had no way to notify me that she wasn't going to be on that plane, and no one could tell her how long it would be before she could get another flight. Seeing her in tears and lips trembling, a guardian angel (actually a wonderful Air Force sergeant) took her in hand, drove her and the kids over to a transient billet that had one crib, one single bed, and a pay phone down the hall. It was the best the sergeant could do. He told Jane how to reach him, and then went back to the air terminal to see what he could do. A little while later, Jane heard the pay phone ringing. She answered it, and it was the sergeant. He told her to get the kids ready, that she was leaving on an earlier flight than the one on which she was originally scheduled. There was no way for her to get the message to me that she would be arriving in Frankfurt earlier than scheduled. Nevertheless, she was elated, and we will be eternally grateful to that Air Force sergeant who owned a caring heart.

Dependents destined for Germany weren't traveling by

passenger jet in 1961. The plane used most frequently was a prop-driven C-118 with the seats turned to the rear. There were stops in Newfoundland, Iceland, and Scotland with the trip taking about 22 hours. One can hardly imagine in 2007 the problems facing a mother with three small children, two of whom were not yet potty-trained, on a plane with only one bathroom and many other young babies on board. It was a tired and weary Army wife that walked off the plane in Frankfurt, Germany, knowing I would not be there to meet her.

It would take a tome to go through the details of how Jane was able to get the word to me that she was already at the Frankfurt airport. When I did get the word, Colonel Bill Weber took much less than an hour to chauffer me down the 60-mile autobahn to the airport. I will forever remember the look on Jane's face and my little girls' faces when I walked into the room where they were waiting. I think I hugged all four of them at the same time. It was a great moment in our lives.

The family would be with me for 26 months in Berlin. We kept our little girls from ever seeing the wall, the concertina, the minefields, and the border guards. No kids were ever kept closer to home. A trip to the post exchange and commissary or to a nearby German pet store was about as far as we ever ventured to take them. A walled-in city where the sun seldom shines and where it snows almost daily during the winter months is not the best place in the world to experience a wholesome family life.

I had over 60 days of leave accumulated and had been given a pay raise by being promoted below the zone to

Major. So, Jane and I decided that we would celebrate our good fortune by taking the kids on a vacation to Bavaria, Austria, and perhaps to Switzerland and Italy. I got all of the paperwork, visas, etc. ready, and we left West Berlin by car in early July of 1963. Once in West Germany, we visited with some old friends and then headed for Bertchesgarten, where we expected to find the sun. We didn't, and after visiting Hitler's Eagles's Nest, the salt mines, and the usual tourist sites, we packed the car and headed over the Brenner Pass to Verona, Italy and Lake Garda. There we found plenty of sun—too much sun, enough in fact that Jane suffered second degree burns and had to be treated at the Army Hospital in Heidelberg on the return trip.

We planned the return trip so as to arrive before noon at Helmstedt on the West German end of the 110-mile autobahn through East Germany to West Berlin. Processing first at the Allied Checkpoint, I drove around the slaloms to the Soviet Checkpoint about 30 yards away, stopped in front of the lift barrier, exited the car, and locked the doors. I walked inside, pushed my papers through a 3-inch high space under a painted glass window and waited. A few minutes later, my papers were returned along with a small piece of paper. The small piece of paper was to be handed to the paramilitary Border Security Policemen (BSP) manning the last lift barrier. I had traveled the autobahn many times and always abided by the Soviet procedure, but this time the barrier was lifted. So, I just drove on through.

About 20 miles down the autobahn, I noticed two East German staff cars approaching from the rear at a high rate of speed. When they caught up with me, one of them passed, then pulled in front and slowed down. The other pulled up beside me on my left. I had been there before—dozens of times in East Berlin. There's nothing to do but stop. We were going to be detained—for what I didn't know. Ordinarily, it would have been part of a normal day, but this time my wife and kids were along. With his rifle cradled in his arms and the barrel pointed at the car, a para-military Border Security Policeman (BSP) came over and laid his hand on the door. I screamed, "Don't touch this car" loudly enough to burst his eardrums, at which time he flinched, and the little girls began to cry. I rolled the window down a few inches and said, "Send me a Soviet officer." One of the other BSPs came over to the car a few minutes later, also cradling his rifle. I gave him the same treatment, as I did the other BSP. This one, however, used the muzzle of his gun to motion us to get out of the car, which of course we were not going to do. I asked again for them to notify a Soviet officer. Moments later, the first BSP to come over to the car moved to within reaching distance of the car, didn't touch it, but motioned for us to unload. It was then that I began to suspect that this was not an unplanned incident.

When detained in East Berlin, I would pour a cup of coffee from my thermos, take out a peanut butter and banana sandwich that I never failed to carry along, and strike up a conversation with my driver—maybe even tell him a joke to get him to laughing. It never failed to frustrate the East Germans. In this instance, we didn't have any coffee or peanut butter sandwiches, and we hadn't eaten since breakfast, but our little girls were too scared to be thinking about food—and Jane was doing all she could to lessen their fright. The BSPS never came back over to the car, but neither did they leave. I think we had waited for about three hours when the American Checkpoint Liaison Officer arrived on the scene. He told me that I had been stopped on orders of the Soviet Checkpoint Officer, because I had failed to surrender the small piece of paper that authorized my travel on the autobahn. I handed him the piece of paper. He winked at me, gave the small slip of paper to the BSPS, and waited for the BSPS to drive away.

It's been over 40 years since that event, but until this writing, I have never leveled with my wife and kids about what our Checkpoint Officer and I always suspected. Colonels Malakov and Sergin, Soviet Checkpoint Officers on each end of the autobahn, knew me very well. The Soviet Commandant in East Berlin, General Solovyev, knew me, too. I had not made life too easy for them, and they were out to get me. I couldn't tell Jane at the time, because she would be worried every time I traveled to East Berlin or had to travel the autobahn. I will never know for certain exactly what they intended to do, but I have absolutely no doubt about whether they had a motive. There would be no way that the East German BSPS would have raised the barrier prior to receiving the travel pass. Also, the BSPS never

L TO R: SHARON LEIGH, MARY ALLEAN, AND KAREN MARIE, AGES 5,8 AND 5 – TOO YOUNG TO UNDERSTAND BEING FORCED OFF THE ROAD, DETAINED FOR SEVERAL HOURS, AND THREATENED AT GUNPOINT BY ANGRY ENEMY SOLDIERS.

motioned me to stop. They wanted me to pass through so that they would have an excuse to stop me. They didn't need the travel pass. It was not a legal document. Its only purpose was to verify to the BSPs that the driver had presented his or her documentation to the Soviets.

Had the BSPs not had a motive, they would not have asked us to get out of the car. Also, if they had simply stopped us, because we hadn't surrendered the travel pass, it logically follows that they would have motioned us to follow them back to the checkpoint. I have no doubt but that their motive was to get us out of the car without breaking into it. Once we were out, they had a host of options. They could haul us away and hold us for any period of time, pump me full of sodium pentothal, try to break me, or threaten to kill my wife and kids if I didn't talk—or all of these and more—anything to get from me any information I had that they wanted. At that time or later, they could tell the U.S. anything. They could deny knowing anything about us. They could elect to accuse me of any kind of a crime, or they could report through diplomatic channels that I had defected to the Soviet Union with my family. In short, nothing good could have come from getting out of the car. You don't ask passengers to get out of a car unless you plan to either do something to them or do something to the car. I didn't think they wanted my car. So, I chose to limit their options to breaking in the car and taking us by force—a bad option for them that they didn't choose to take.

Upon arriving back at Berlin Brigade Headquarters, I had a stack of mail to wade through, among which was the good news that I would be departing in December 1963 for the Armed Forces Staff College at Norfolk, Virginia—six months earlier than I had expected to leave Berlin. The day before we were to take the "Duty Train" to Frankfurt, I got a call from someone, who wouldn't identify himself on the phone, telling me that they were taking a little extra precaution to see that we had a safe trip. I don't know what they did or what prompted their concern, but I thought it extremely unusual. Over the years, I have reflected upon the autobahn incident and the telephone call, and it causes me to know that I had been gambling with the lives of my Army wife and three little children.

From a professional point of view, the six months at Norfolk weren't worth much. We learned a few things about our sister services but nothing that we couldn't have learned from the printed page. All of the services—Army, Navy, Air Force, Marines—were equally represented, and we gained a lot of new friendships that have endured the test of time.

Looking through the scrapbooks we put together in those years is entertainment on one hand and saddening on the other. We had learned before leaving Berlin that Sharon's vision in one eye had been impaired during delivery. The only hope the optometrist gave us was to have her wear a patch over her good eye in hope that it would strengthen the weak one. During all of our time at Norfolk, Sharon wore that patch. With a patch covering her good eye, she had to find her way along and couldn't keep up on a walk. The patch didn't do what the optometrist had hoped. In fact, the good eye grew weaker through lack of use—just another painful time in the plight of an Army wife.

About half way through the course, I received word

that I was being assigned to the Pentagon for a three-year tour with Infantry Branch. It was an honor I was told to be picked for the assignment, and the fact that I would be there for three years led us to look toward buying our first house rather than rent an apartment. We went looking the next weekend and found a nice split level house in Springfield, Virginia, owned by a Marine Major and his wife. They had financed the house with a VA loan and would have preferred any other arrangement except our assuming the loan. As unfair as the regulations might have been, the original owner was never freed of responsibility until the VA loan was paid back. Nevertheless, they agreed to our paying their equity and assuming the loan. In order to do that, we needed $2,200, which we didn't have, but we were able to come up with the money by cashing in all of our War Bonds, borrowing on an insurance policy, and spending absolutely no money except for food. We went to settlement, and the house was ours.

When the day arrived for us to leave Norfolk, we cleared out our checking account from a local bank and headed to Springfield with a total of $400 that Jane tucked away in her purse. We had planned to use that to buy a washing machine and enough food to last us until payday. That didn't happen either. We hadn't eaten all day, and the kids were complaining of being hungry, which we knew they were. So, I opted to go to get us some hamburgers or something, but when Jane went to get some money from her purse, she discovered that she had about $25 left. One of the movers had stolen the money. Again, this was not a joyful time in the life of an Army wife, but we managed to get to the end of the month by getting a few dollars of advanced pay.

My initial job in Infantry Branch was to handle the assignments of newly-commissioned Second Lieutenants from West Point, ROTC, and OCS. Assignments to Vietnam and to units being formed for divisions and brigades being deployed to Vietnam drew first priority. Even yet, I don't know who to blame specifically for setting the length of a tour in Vietnam at one-year, but it would have taken a caucus of geniuses working in concert to figure out a worse decision. It was an assignment officer's nightmare, and I know it cost us dearly in combat effectiveness and I suspect in human life as well. As I write this, I can't find a word to describe the devastating effects of the turnover of officer leadership. To make matters worse, somebody decided that Lieutenant Colonels in the Combat Arms (Infantry, Armor, and Artillery) should command a battalion for only six months in Vietnam and then do something else. Movement of officers to and from Vietnam was so fast and furious that we literally destroyed the effectiveness of every division in Europe and elsewhere. We had the highest percentage of officers in transit in the history of the Army.

Looking back upon it, there was nothing complicated about the job of being an assignment officer. It simply took long hours at the office, assigning officers to locations all over the world and making trips to the various units and schools throughout the country. Little time was left for the wife and family. What would have ordinarily been a great time for an Army wife seemed no different to Jane.

Career military officers exist for the purpose of fighting the nation's wars. They neither start them nor cause them, but when one does start, every officer who is worth his salt believes that he should be where the action is—not because he loves war but because he believes that he can beat the enemy with the least possible loss of human life. I volunteered in writing for Vietnam in 1965, but it would be May of 1967 before my time would come. I had made Lieutenant Colonel by then and looked forward to commanding a battalion in Vietnam. I knew what wars were like, and the wife and kids knew something about them, too. The TV had brought the Vietnam War into the living rooms across America. It was not an easy thing for the wife and kids to say goodbye, knowing that they may never see me again. It wasn't any easier for me, either. I loved them beyond description, and I could not be sure that they would be OK. I'll never forget the tears and their holding on for just that last second. I learned one thing that day that I now know to be true and indisputable: Fighting a war is not nearly so tough as the mental and emotional stress known to the wife and kids of the ones who do it. I spent the flight to Vietnam thinking of them and not the war I was going to fight.

The tough thing about leaving for Vietnam had nothing to do with the war. In fact, every officer who's worth his salt wants to be where the action is. However, about four months earlier, we had noticed bruises starting to appear all over 6-year old Karen's little body. She looked like a victim of child abuse. We took her to DeWitt Army Hospital at Fort Belvoir, Virginia, where a blood test revealed that she had only about 3.0 percent of the needed number of red blood platelets. The doctor's first act was to conduct a spinal tap to either verify or rule out leukemia. It was prayer time, and we spent the waiting period doing it. The doctor's tests showed that the bone marrow was producing healthy platelets, but they were being killed off by her spleen. His decision to give her steroids to deactivate the spleen, check her platelet content bi-weekly, administer steroids as needed, and keep doing it as often as necessary until I completed a tour in Vietnam. An operation to remove the spleen would be performed as soon as I returned. The plan worked, but during that year, Karen could play no games, ride a tricycle with other kids, get on a swing, or do anything else that might cause her to fall or bump any part of her body. Jane had to be with her every waking moment.

Midway through a tour in Vietnam, one could make provisions for six days of rest and recuperation at one of several places in the Pacific. I chose to meet Jane in Hawaii in December of 1967, and the greatest writer to ever hold a pen couldn't begin to describe how wonderful those six days were. When they ended, I stood outside the airport and watched her plane disappear into the clouds. It was pouring rain, and I was soaking wet, but I didn't care. I had gotten used to it in 'Nam. In fact, I didn't have time to change clothes before boarding a plane headed in the opposite direction.

I was fortunate to be in 'Nam during the first five months of 1968. The North Vietnamese Army and the Viet Cong kicked off their most widespread action of the war, later termed the "Tet Offensive." We put a terrible beating on the enemy all over South Vietnam, and I personally felt that I paid the Army back for what they invested in me. Even the Comptroller General couldn't deny me that. All of us learned later, though, that somehow or other the enemy was the big winner. The American press as well as millions of Americans turned their backs on us all, and our families back home bore the brunt of it. Anti-war activists went so far as to call our wives and children and tell them such things as "We just thought that you might like to know that your husband/father has been singled out by North Vietnam. He will come home in a body bag." I had seen anti-war, anti-military sentiment during the Korean War, but I was not prepared for what I saw when I returned from Vietnam. It was not a fun time to be a soldier or an Army wife.

On my return from Vietnam, I spent a year at Fort Benning, helping to prepare other soldiers to fight the unique war that was Vietnam. One of the first things we did on arriving there was to take Karen to the hospital, anticipating an operation to remove her spleen. The doctors, however, decided to give her one last round of steroids. Miraculously, when they took her off the steroids, her blood count remained at just below average. In answer to our fervent prayer, her blood count remains to this day at acceptable levels.

We had rented our house in Springfield, anticipating that we would probably have to return to the Washington area at a future time. There was a lot of uncertainty, as there always is for an Army family. By now, though, I had begun to see a different look in Jane's eyes. Not only had the better life that I had promised her not happened, but now we found ourselves being hated by our own countrymen. The majority of the American people had not been able to differentiate between a war they hated and those who were sent to fight it. Soldiers and their families had cause to conclude that the nation they served had dealt them a bad hand.

About six months after arriving at Fort Benning, I was notified that I had been selected to attend the Army War College at Carlisle Barracks, Pennsylvania. Ordinarily, that would be a cause to celebrate, but I didn't see it that way at the time. I felt certain that it was the next step enroute to another tour in the Pentagon—the last place on earth I wanted to be assigned. Moreover, it meant packing up and moving again, something that we had just completed doing. Incidentally, we made a lot of moves that in the interest of shortening a long story I have elected not to discuss, and something bad seemed to happen on each occasion. There were three moves in Berlin, and there would be three moves at Carlisle. How Jane and other Army wives kept their sanity is something about which I continue to marvel.

A few days after we arrived at Carlisle, General Omar Bradley came to the War College to be present for the formal opening of the Bradley Museum. It just so happened that an estimated mob of 30,000 anti-war demonstrators showed up the same day, their purpose being in part to interfere with the occasion. The circumference of Carlisle Barracks is only about a mile, and all entrances and exits were blocked. My oldest daughter, Mary, then 13, had a piano lesson about a mile from the post. Jane had some misgivings, and so did I, but we were both determined that she was going to make it. I put her in the car and headed out one of the gates only to be blocked by a mass of humanity. I stepped out of the car and said in a rather loud voice, "My daughter has a piano lesson that I don't intend for her to miss. Now, if you Viet Cong don't have enough brains to get out of the road, you've got a problem, because I'm going to drive my daughter to her piano lesson." I got in the car and started forward. A young man yelled to the crowd to "Get back!" They started moving, and I drove through, brushing against several of them in the process. I dropped her off at her piano teacher's house, came back to the base, went back after her in a couple of hours, picked her up, and returned, each time by the same route. On each occasion, they yelled and screamed obscenities, but they cleared a path for me to pass. I mentioned the event only to ask rhetorically how a father can answer a 13-year old daughter's question when she says, "Daddy, these people are from America. Why do they hate us?" I know she didn't understand, but the only thing I remember saying to her was "I don't know, but it's like going over to your school to protest some rule and beat the janitor half to death. They're uneducated as to our system of government and are taking their anger out on the wrong people." To this and to so many other similar things, Jane often remarked that "It looks like we could just be able to live a normal life."

The year at the Army War College was almost like a vacation on active duty. Others may not have considered it as such, but there was no night work, no examinations, no extensive study requirements. We did have an Individual Research Paper to write, but we were permitted to choose the subject. Most of the morning hours were spent by listening to a distinguished guest speaker, followed by an hour or so of questions and answers, and the rest of the day spent doing seminar work or conducting research. I was able to spend more time with Jane and the girls than during any four or five other years combined. The good times would end, however, in June of 1970. It was back to the Pentagon for four years with the Army General Staff and Joint Chiefs of Staff, and the odds of seeing my kids awake on any given day was less than 50–50. The task of raising the children fell almost exclusively to an Army wife who had little help from her husband. He wasn't there when she needed him.

The last four years of our time in the military were spent at the University of Alabama as Professor of Military Science (PMS). Even there, I was usually not available. My summers were spent at Fort Riley, Kansas, and because we had experienced some recruiting success at the University of Alabama, the Army sent me around the country helping other programs with their recruitment effort. In the meantime, Jane kept waiting for the great family life that lay at the end of the rainbow.

Memorial Day and Veterans Day have been set aside to remember those who have died in the service of our country and to honor those who have served in all wars. Borrowing a line from Lincoln, it "is altogether fitting and proper that we should do this." We set aside a day to honor all mothers and a day to honor all fathers, whether some deserve to be honored or not. We set aside a day to honor certain people by name, and we set aside a day to honor all people who work. It would also be "altogether fitting and proper" to set aside a day to honor a group just as deserving of credit as those mentioned above: the wives of career soldiers.

It should be obvious by now that the author is a follower of Jesus Christ. I am thankful to Him for letting me serve my country in uniform for over 32 years. I am thankful to Him for letting me know what it's like to serve both as an officer and an enlisted man. I thank Him for giving me the courage, integrity, and ability to fulfill my duty to my country, the Army, and to the men I led. I thank Him for letting me reach the grade of Colonel, and most of all, I thank Him for making me a Private in His army and showing me that one can be a soldier of the cross as well as of the flag. His army is an all-volunteer force, and there is no Selective Service draft, no age limitations, no disqualifying physical profile. He has provided a perfect retirement plan and an eternal home of incomparable beauty—both absolutely free to each and every member of His army without regard to length of service.

Just who is this man whom I credit with having done all of these things? I could never end this book without telling the reader about Him. He is my dearest friend, and He holds the key to the future of America and the world. A stronger, safer, and better America is not possible without Him.

WHO IS THE MAN NAMED JESUS?

In the beginning was the Word, and the Word was with God, and the Word was God. The same was in the beginning with God. All things were made by him, and without him was not anything made that was made.

—John 1:1—3 (KJV, The Holy Bible)

GOD MAY NEVER HAVE INTENDED FOR MAN TO understand everything contained in The Holy Bible. It is obvious, however, that he did intend for it to contain an inexhaustible supply of spiritual food. In that respect, there is no other book quite like it. Unlike all other books or volumes of books that man can read and master, The Holy Bible stands alone as the one book in which the same passage conveys to the serious reader a new and deeper insight each time that one turns to its pages for spiritual nourishment. If anyone doubts that The Holy Bible is the inspired word of God, he or she needs only to try and comprehend all that it says and teaches. He or she will learn something new and deepen their understanding day after day and year after year, and the more they learn from it the more there is left to learn. Only God could have put such a unique masterpiece in print.

The words in the The Holy Bible cry out to us, telling us to seek God's wisdom, to obey His commandments, and give Him complete control of our lives. Early on in the very first chapter of the Bible, we are introduced to His intriguing multiplicity—unlimited omnipotence, omnipresence, and omniscience. "Let Us make man in Our image, after Our likeness," God said (Genesis 2:26, KJV, The Holy Bible). As page after page of the Bible unfolds, we learn of God the Father, God the Son, and God the Holy Spirit—three manifestations of the same God, the one God, the only God—with only God the Son having revealed Himself to us as a visible, physical being.

The roles of God the Son and God the Holy Spirit in Old Testament times escape many otherwise great scholars of the Bible, but both are active throughout. Standing in the way of our understanding of God the Son (or Christ Jesus) is the mistaken view that man is a physical being who owns an immortal soul. Instead, we must understand at the outset that man is a spiritual being, just like the angels, except that we temporarily occupy a perishable physical body. The spirit is immortal. Only the physical body dies, and at the moment of the death of the physical body, there is cause to believe that man never loses consciousness. He or she is either escorted by the angels into Paradise or incarcerated in what I Peter 3:19 of the King James Version of the Holy Bible refers to as a "prison" and will remain there until the day of judgment, which will happen a thousand years plus after the second-coming of Christ (Chapter 20, Book of Revelation, the Holy Bible).

Explaining all that the Bible says about Jesus is a tall order for even the most learned of scholars. It is, however, my belief that the Scriptures reveal enough about the things we can't understand to enable us to talk about them to Christian friends as well as to the unsaved who do not have a personal relationship with Christ Jesus.

There are things I don't understand about the Bible and the Trinity, and yet there are things I know for certain. I know that Jesus is real, that He governs my life more than any other person or thing, that He is the Sovereign God of this world, and that He is mankind's only avenue of escape from eternal incarceration in the depths of hell.

The Bible calls Jesus by many names. He is the *Messiah*, the *Savior*, the *Everlasting Father*, the *Prince of Peace*, the *Son of Man*, the *Son of God*, the *Lamb of God*, *God's Only Begotten Son*, and *Lord* among others. Some of these—*Son of Man, Son of God*, and *God's Only Begotten Son*—have given rise to false theologies like those espoused by Jehovah's Witnesses and those who relegate Jesus to a position lower than God. Those who have made this fatal error have tried to understand the Trinity of God in physical terms. This has led them to believe there are three gods, some to conclude that the Trinity is impossible, and even others to contend that Jesus and the Holy Spirit are subordinate to God. These false theologies must of course be rejected, because they have been developed by men who have never come to grips with the spiritual truth of the Trinity and are thus destined from the outset to arrive at a false and erroneous conclusion.

The word "Trinity" does not appear in the Scriptures, and there is no single exposition of it in either the *Old* or the *New Testament*. Yet, it is a clearly inferred doctrine that flows so freely from the total Biblical message that a single exposition of it is not required. God has revealed enough of it to us for all to know its great truth.

First, the Bible tells us that Jesus existed before the creation of the world. In fact, if we believe the truth of the Trinity, then we have to conclude without question that Jesus has always existed. Now, all we can do is to view that great and mind-boggling truth with awesome wonder, because man is incapable of understanding anything that doesn't have a beginning. We don't fully understand eternity either, but we can talk about it and accept its truth by simple faith. To do that, we must embrace the premise that God started time and that there will be a time when He will end it. When that time comes, *all physical things and all mankind will enter eternity—a timeless existence free of all negative things that time had previously caused to happen. From that moment on, aging will cease in the Kingdom of Heaven and the depths of hell.* Understanding how this can happen transcends the greatest of human minds, and that's surely one of the reasons why Solomon, with all of his wisdom, cautioned us in Proverbs 3:5 to "lean not on your own understanding."

The words "us" and "our" used by God in Genesis 1:26 are plural to the physical-minded, but to the spiritually-minded Christian, they are singular as well as plural. We must therefore conclude that the Trinity of God is the Creator of the world. However, God the Son was the specific part of the Trinity that God used in creating the world and all that it holds (John 1:3 & Colossians 1:16–17).

Sunday School teachers often err in their attempts to explain the Trinity in human terms using physical examples. Church goers have heard the Trinity likened unto a rope with three strands, or to a triform of interlocking circles, or to the head of a company who functions as President, Chief Executive Officer, and Chairman of the Board. But these and all others fall short of illustrating the Trinity, because two of the three manifestations of God are wholly spiritual, and each person of the Trinity is the whole of Himself while at the same instant being fully the other two. Such multi-existence is too much for the human mind to comprehend, let alone being able to understand the fact that God has the power to instantaneously remove forgiven sin from His memory while at the same time having the incomprehensible power to selectively give knowledge to one manifestation of His being while denying it to the others. Only God the Father knows the moment of the second coming of Christ Jesus (Matthew 24:36, *The Holy Bible*). Similarly, inasmuch as the Trinity is perfectly holy and completely just, the Trinity decided in the beginning to withhold all knowledge from Themselves as to who would and wouldn't accept Jesus as Lord and Savior. If God permitted Himself to foreknow who would accept Him, the mind of sinful man would lead him to assert that *"No just God would let me be born into the world knowing I would spend eternity in the depths of hell."* The Bible doesn't tell us this, but there is a message that flows throughout the Scriptures warning us that anything that makes God less than perfect must be rejected as false theology. Summarily, the Trinity is too complex to be likened unto any comparisons that mankind can manufacture. The functions of all human or physical examples are limited to location, while the Trinity of God permeates all creation to the infinite depths of space. This is a relationship that transcends human reason at any level of scholarly achievement. The bottom line is that God knows what He chooses to know. *Don't try to understand it. Just accept its eternal truth by simple faith.*

We are told in John 1:18 that no one has seen God. There are those who want to argue that this passage contradicts other passages in the Scriptures, including Jesus' own statement that "I and the Father are One"—that if anyone had seen Him they had seen the Father. There is, of course, no contradiction. What Jesus was saying is that God has not chosen to manifest Himself visually to us as God the Father. He has on the other hand chosen to manifest Himself to us visually as God the Son, and it is my personal interpretation of the Scriptures that He has chosen to do this since the creation of man.

I have never heard it said by anyone. Nor have I read it in any book, but it is obvious to me that it was Christ Jesus who communed with Adam and Eve in the Garden of Eden. If not, then God the Father signaled His presence with the sound of footsteps. It is likewise logical that it was God the Son Who, according to Genesis 17:1, "*appeared*" to Abram and identified Himself as Almighty God. It likewise logically follows that it was Christ Jesus who dined with Abraham and Sarah. It's just that God the Son did not at that time bear the name of Jesus Christ .

The first chapter of John deals with the identity of Jesus and likewise identifies Him as the Creator of the world. In these verses, John does not mention the Trinity by name but nevertheless speaks of two of the Three Persons of God. In Verse 1 of Chapter 1, John relates that "In the beginning was the Word, and the Word was with God, and the Word was God." "Word" in each instance is capitalized. It comes from the Greek word "Logos," which in Greek is both a verb and a noun, but John used it as a title for Christ Jesus. If one then substitutes the name "Jesus" in place of "Word," the verse's meaning cannot escape the attention and understanding of the hastiest of readers. *"In the beginning was Jesus, and Jesus was with God, and Jesus was God."* Its truth and meaning could not be stated more clearly. Jesus is God.

John goes on to say in Verse 2 that Jesus was with God in the beginning (meaning the beginning of the creation of the world—not God's beginning). In Verse 3 John identifies Jesus as the Creator of the world. Then, if one at that point has any doubt that John is talking about God the Son, he clarifies it in Verse 14 in stating that "the Word (Jesus) was made flesh and dwelt among us."

The Apostle Paul further amplifies Jesus' role as the Creator of everything in Verses 15 through 19 of the 1st Chapter of Colossians. Paul writes that "He (meaning Jesus) is the image of the invisible God, the "first-born of all creation" (translated "preeminence"—not an actual birth). "For by Him all things were created: things in heaven and things on earth, visible and invisible, whether thrones, or powers or rulers or authorities; all things were created by Him and for Him. He is before all things, and in Him all things hold together; and He is the Head of the body, the church; He is the beginning and the first-born among the dead, so that in everything He might have supremacy; for God was pleased to have His fullness in Him." Special note needs to be taken here. The fullness of God, the total God, all that is God is in Christ Jesus.

One might then ask, why did God need to manifest Himself to us as God the Son? Why not just God the Father? Well, due to man's sin, God in his infinite mercy and saving grace chose to reconcile Himself to the world through His own physical death as God the Son upon the Cross of Calvary. Through the shedding of His blood, man's sin could be remitted., and God the Son could thereafter bridge the gap between God the Father and man that would otherwise have been an eternal barrier between sinful man and a just and holy God. Man had to become sinless in God's eyes, and this could only happen through the shedding of blood. This explains the reason for the incarnation, for Jesus' life and ministry, for His betrayal and crucifixion, and for His resurrection from the grave.

Almost as difficult to understand as the Trinity is the *incarnation* of Christ, but an understanding of it is essential if we are to understand how Jesus could be fully God and fully man. He knew every pain, every sorrow, every emotion, and every temptation known to man, and yet he was without sin—and at the same time He remained completely holy and completely just.

Now, how could all of that be possible? The Four Gospels and the many books by Paul make it clear that the incarnation was a merciful act of God, whereby God took our human nature into union with His divine person. He thus became the "Incarnate God" which is synonymous with "God's Only Begotten Son." No birth in all of history has ever been like it, because only a part of Jesus was born. The Divine Person of the union was not born. He already existed. There appears to be only one explanation that the human mind can comprehend and only one word in the English language to describe it. That word is "hypostatical," meaning that the two natures were not in any way mixed or confounded but rather remained individually personal and separate. In that way, Jesus became fully man while remaining fully God. Then in some wonderful and intriguing way, the union remained spiritually permanent, because we know that Jesus ascended into Heaven with the same body that lay dead for three days in the tomb—a body that looked the same with a capability to consume food and drink but also imperishable and unrestricted by barriers, time, and space.

Summarily then, who is the man named Jesus? He is God the Father, God the Son, and God the Holy Spirit—and He came into the world—not to condemn it but to save it—to be delivered voluntarily to the cross *to die in our place for our offenses and to be raised again for our "justification"*—a word denoting a judicial act of God by which He pardons all of the sins of those who believe in Christ Jesus, place their trust in Him, and surrender to His lordship. God treats the believer as *righteous* in the eyes of the law. In addition to God's action to pardon man's sin, He declares that all of the provisions of His law have been satisfied. *Justification* is therefore the act of *The Supreme Judge of All Creation* and not that of a sovereign. In declaring a believer to be *justified* or *righteous*, God is not relaxing or setting aside His holy law but is declaring it instead to be fulfilled in its strictest sense. *Justified* man is thus entitled to all of the advantages and rewards arising from perfect obedience to the law. *Justification* is not the forgiveness of a person without righteousness. It is instead a declaration that the justified person possesses a righteousness which perfectly and eternally satisfies every provision of God's law. The sole condition on which righteousness is credited is the believer's faith (repenting, trusting, and giving Christ complete control of one's life). Jesus is therefore *"the Way, the Truth and the Life."* He is the alter-ego of God the Father and God the Holy Spirit, and in His own words He tells us that we cannot come to God the Father, except through Him.

Those who believe in Jesus and repent of their sinful nature, place their complete and total trust in Him, and surrender to Him as the Lord of their lives (in the process rejecting Satan as their master) will through His wonderful saving grace inherit eternal life with the Trinity in Heaven. He will forgive their sins. Though guilty, He will declare them not guilty. Their names will be recorded in the Lamb's Book of Life along with all others who have received His saving grace.

How do we know that all of this is true? Well, we know it through the internal change that has occurred within us. We are new creatures who have undergone a spiritual rebirth (John 3:7 and 2 Corinthians 5:17) and are being transformed to His image (Romans 8:29). Moreover, Jesus said it, and every true follower of Christ knows that is enough to make it so.

Satan knows for certain that everything written here about Christ Jesus is true. It therefore logically follows that simply believing that Jesus is everything He professes to be is in and of itself insufficient to receive His saving grace. Jesus Himself warns us in Matthew 7:21 that: "Not everyone who sayeth unto me 'Lord Lord' shall enter the Kingdom of Heaven, but he that doeth the will of My Father Which is in Heaven."

Satan himself is a believer, but there's something that he has not done—and cannot do. He has committed the unpardonable sin and cannot and will not repent, place his trust in Jesus, and surrender to His Lordship. Satan also knows his final destination—a place called "hell" where there will be the hottest of flames that will burn eternally but give off no light. Misery loves company, and that old serpent obviously wants billions in his future home of everlasting darkness. He is history's best liar, and being far more cunning than any unsaved mortal man, he is able to peddle his two greatest lies with near limitless success. He makes those who have never given their lives to Christ Jesus think that they have plenty of time to make a profession of faith. He also causes them to believe that he can outdo God Almighty in providing a life of joy and happiness on earth. Every day that he delays someone in committing their life to Christ Jesus, he wins—and that person loses—maybe eternally. There is no good reason why any sane person should not be willing to accept God's free gift of eternal life, and yet Satan is able to lure many of the world's greatest scientific minds into his kingdom and use them to help him spread atheism and immorality to all mankind. Surely, their naivety and evil intentions rank first and second among the wonders of the world.

The souls of thousands will be required of them the very day that the reader finishes this book. My fervent prayer is that physical death will not precede spiritual rebirth for any reader of these words.

If you do not know Jesus Christ as your personal savior, go to Him in prayer. Confess that you are a sinner, that you are sorry for your sin, and ask for His forgiveness. Tell Him that you want to turn from sin and turn to Him and ask His help in doing it. You can't do it on your own. Tell Him that you are placing your trust in Him and giving Him control of your life. Then, thank Jesus for saving your soul and commit yourself to profess Him publicly through baptism and church membership. Do not let a Sunday pass until you have kept your promise at a church where Jesus Christ is Lord.

EPILOGUE

THE AUTHOR RECOGNIZES THAT THIS BOOK DOES not contain everything that will help build a stronger, safer, and better America. I do, however, assert that every part of this book will in some way contribute to that end. I have tried to select subject areas that I believe to be essential to the future of America. Atheists and perhaps members of other religious beliefs may take issue with the emphasis I have placed on observance of Judeo-Christian principles. If so, I am prepared to receive their criticism. I am also prepared to question their motives.

Why an atheist, misguided judge, court of law, politician, or some American Civil Liberties Union (ACLU) activist would want to convince others that God is a myth or that the mention of His name in a public place violates someone's civil rights is mind-boggling. A true Christian owns an impeccable moral character. He or she obeys the law, loves and seeks to help their neighbor, and comes to the aid of the needy. They neither lie, cheat, steal, nor seek to harm society in any way. They don't force their beliefs on anybody, and neither does the God they serve. He gives mankind a freedom to choose Him or reject Him.

I would never want to see Darwin, Roman, or Greek Mythology banned from the classroom. Professors should teach about them and call them what they are. The whole world knows that Roman and Greek Mythology are what their title says they are. Darwin's Theory of Evolution is what its title suggests it is. It is theory, not indisputable established truth, and it is a violation of the Scientific Method and intellectual honesty to teach it as fact. Moreover, no student should ever be punished with a lower grade if he or she rejects it. Creation by chance or creation by choice is an *exclusive alternative* that every student has a right to choose without penalty. A professor has a right to state that he or she believes in Darwin's Theory of Evolution, but they must admit in doing it that theirs is a faith statement—just as a believer in Creation by Choice must admit that their belief is based on simple faith in the validity of the Scriptures.

Before anyone rejects the spiritual condition of the American people as being essential to a stronger, safer, and better America, I ask them to listen to the testimony of any believer who became a Christian after reaching adulthood or simply talk to his or her family, friends, and acquaintances. Pay careful attention to what the person was like before his or her conversion and how their character and behavior underwent a complete metamorphosis after becoming a Christian. Even many atheists will not deny that a true conversion to Christianity by every American would in time empty our jails and prisons, take the locks off our doors, negate the need for a police force, and put trial lawyers out of business. Such a dream is beyond reach in our lifetime, but a stronger, safer, and better America is well within our grasp as long as we remember that *evil and everything bad for mankind exist only where God isn't.*

Help us to tell others about this book. If it changed your life, tell them how and ask them to join you as a member of the American Patriotism Association. Do some high school student or good friend a wonderful favor by making a gift of it, asking him or her to read it carefully, and give you their reaction.

It is my fervent hope that you will keep this book by your bedside, refer to it often, and recommend it to others. All monies from its sale or any membership dues paid to the American Patriotism Association will be used to operate the Association, fund its charitable causes, and aid in building a stronger, safer, and better America.

Who Should Become a
Member of the American
Patriotism Association?

MEN AND WOMEN OF A COMMON MORAL FIBER bind themselves together. The American Patriotism Association (APA) is such an assembly. Heretofore, there has never been an organization in America that identifies every true patriot from every walk of life, ethnic group, national origin, educational background, and occupation. It's intent is to benefit the whole of America and to bring every truly patriotic American under a great umbrella of love and loyalty to the United States of America. As the Association embarks upon this noble undertaking, it does so under the premise that when apprised of the existence of the APA and its purposes every true patriot will join its ranks.

Joining the American Patriotism Association is a statement that one is a patriotic American, loyal to the nation's institutions and ideals, a law-abiding citizen, a person of impeccable moral character, and a citizen of the United States committed to preserving our way of life for Americans yet unborn. The APA enables its members to proudly place their names among the true patriots of America—men and women who will never dishonor the United States of America either by word or deed.

Membership dues/purchase of this book permit the APA to:

» Provide scholarships to deserving young Americans with priority to dependents of APA members.

» Contribute significant financial gifts to humanitarian and patriotic foundations, charities and ministries.

» Produce materials that will assist parents and teachers in educating this and future generations of young Americans about the traditions, ideals, and principles that have made and kept America free, inculcating and instilling in them the basic ingredients, habits, and behavior of a truly responsible and patriotic citizenry.

One can join the American Patriotism Association on the internet (www.americanpatriotism.com) using a Visa, MasterCard, or American Express Credit Card or by sending a check (payable to APA) in the amount of $20 to:

The American Patriotism Association

2070 Valleydale Road, Suite 2

Birmingham, Alabama 35244